SCHOLASTIC

Teaching
Real-Life Nonfiction
Reading Skills
in the K-1 Classroom

Barbara S. Pinto

New York • Toronto • London • Auckland • Sydney
Mexico City • New Delhi • Hong Kong • Buenos Aires

Teaching *Resources*

Acknowledgments

How can I sum up the angels in my life? I have learned that nothing is done alone, including writing. Since first grade I have written poetry. Yet, as a mother, wife, teacher, coach, and mentor, I wrote only for school, a parent newsletter, or shared curriculum for the school system.

That all changed when I joined Colleen Cruz's inspiring professional writing group, filled with talented New York City teachers. On our cozy Wednesday evenings, I found my writer's voice. A small ocean of ideas made its way into this book; cohesive and thorough, thanks to Colleen, Theresa, Priya, Connie, Sarah, Kristin, Kerri, Australia (and Nadine's snacks). My mainstay group—you rock!

Along the way there were "prodders"—Lauren Fontana, Amy Santucci, Daniel Kim, Norah Greenstein, Carmen Farina, Sarah Picard, Dan Feigelson, Kathy Collins, Carl Anderson, Pam Allyn, Ellyn Roberson, Laura Kotch, and countless educators who convinced me my message was worth writing. And a giant thank-you to Lucy Calkins, who helped fuel my fire for writing in so many ways.

Others continue to share their faith in me—teachers at my most recent school, PS 6 (especially Barbara Rosenblum and Rebecca Applebaum, whom I learn from daily), and my Scholastic friends, Virginia Dooley and my incredible editors, Joanna Davis-Swing and Sarah Glasscock. I rely on this brain trust for innovation, ruthless honesty, and encouragement. My countless students continually challenge and motivate me to think deeply and creatively. Thanks, too, to teachers Rebecca Satten, Angela Beck, and others who have allowed me to experiment with their students.

My sons, Matt and Greg (my teachers!), cheer me on. Their anecdotes are sprinkled throughout these pages. Most profoundly of all, I thank my insightful husband, Rory, who lets me express myself, holds my hand during meltdowns, provides feedback (solicited or not!), and (even without prompting) checks my grammar. His patience, love, and support overwhelm me daily.

I feel truly blessed to have you all in my life.

Cover design: Jorge J. Namerow
Cover photograph: © Bigstock (boy), © Veer (seed packet)
Interior photographs: Matt Pinto
Interior illustrations: Greg Harris, Rusty Fletcher, and Maxie Chambliss
Interior design: Melinda Belter
Development Editor: Joanna Davis-Swing
Editor: Sarah Glasscock
Copyeditor: David Klein

ISBN: 978-0-545-35392-2
Copyright © 2013 by Barbara S. Pinto
All rights reserved.
Printed in the U.S.A.

1 2 3 4 5 6 7 8 9 10 11 12   40   20 19 18 17 16 15 14 13

Contents

Learn why informational text is vital in today's early education, the research behind nonfiction reading and writing, and specific skills and strategies.

Students embark on a "learning walk" to notice environmental print around school and realize why words matter.

Children sort snacks using a food guide and design their own healthy eating placemats, while they build vocabulary and learn good eating habits.

Students examine newsletters from varied sources to help them create an informational school newsletter with nonfiction features. Showcase related materials in the world to serve as nonfiction mentors.

Children learn map skills by completing an active treasure hunt. They use maps and map keys to navigate and study their school or neighborhood.

Introduction

My Journey

When I was six, I lined up my dolls and played school. My imaginary chalkboard was my first "classroom," where I began my long educational career. After twenty-five years of teaching in early childhood classrooms and nine years as a literacy coach and consultant, I've gained insight about how children learn best.

We want our teaching to be authentic, to come *from* the world, and to prepare our students *for* the world. This book draws on my life experiences both in and out of the classroom. Much of what I have learned comes from being a parent, as well as a lifelong educator.

Each of the seven adventures presented here is a compilation of my work with brilliant teachers, precocious children, and exciting curricula. I have learned from the "stars" as well as the novices about ways to construct ideas for an integrated curriculum that addresses what children really want and need.

Six Pillars of Good Teaching

After watching countless educational approaches come and go, I realize that the pillars of good teaching are universal, not program-based. The following six pillars underlie *Teaching Real-Life Nonfiction Reading Skills in the K–1 Classroom:*

1. **Good Teaching Is Intrinsically Motivating and Based on Personal Interests:** Motivating students is a necessary start for good teaching. Motivation leads to engagement and increased learning.

   Although children have different interests, fun is the biggest energizer. For a five- or six-year-old, another big motivator is "ME, ME, ME." Developmentally, young children's interests are rooted in themselves. While some favor baseball and others ballet, children who have personal choice and find their passion connect easily with learning.

   Tapping into personal interests is essential. Let's face it, even as adults, we enjoy looking at our own vacation photos more than anyone else's! In real-life adventures, such as the activities in this book, we find situations that children care about to promote learning.

2. **Good Teaching Provides Authentic and Practical Experiences:** What is more real than learning about the world we live in? Educators used to believe that children first learn to read and then read to learn. Theorists now believe that learning and reading go hand in hand. Informational texts comprise most of students' reading, in and out of the classroom, including standardized tests. We can simulate life outside the classroom to benefit our students' learning. Beyond nonfiction books, real activities drawn from students' day-to-day lives provide an ever-invigorating source of nonfiction learning.

   You may read some of these chapters, and think, "Of course!"—it is almost too obvious that these activities are the basis for teaching so many skills. As teachers, we learn to mine our everyday world for material to support our students' acquisition of nonfiction reading and writing skills.

3. **Good Teaching Involves Repetition and Practice:** "Read it again!" That was my son Matt's lively cry as I turned the last page of his bedtime story. Multiple readings lead to word retention and language development, and kids love to hear them.

   Research now verifies what parents and teachers know instinctively. Michael Tipper likens memories to footpaths that become overgrown, and repeated patterns help us recall and acquire new vocabulary. In this book, you'll find repeated practice through multiple methods, such as sorting, creating books, and rereading.

4. **Good Teaching Builds Independence and Self-Esteem:** When my son Greg was five, he taught himself to stop his bike by crashing into a soft bush! It took him two hours of "bush-stopping" to get it. He was beaming with pride from ear to ear: "I did it!" Hard work creates a sense of mastery and self-sufficiency. Independence builds self-esteem.

   As teachers, we create safe environments to allow children to fall before they stand, to inquire and explore. From tying shoelaces to opening snacks, they learn at their own pace. Independence is a road to proficiency and pride in accomplishment.

5. **Good Teaching Provides Continued Learning Through a Strong Home-School Connection:** When we invite parents to be educational partners, students achieve greater academic success. At-home practice provides reinforcement through repetition and engagement. Parents often want to help but don't know how or have little time. So we can offer *simple* and *lighthearted* ideas—manageable ideas for concrete follow-up and a review of concepts. Parents are instrumental in reading aloud—*the most effective way to develop more proficient readers.* One of our greatest tools is the power of example.

6. **Good Teaching Lays the Groundwork for Upper-Grade Informational Reading:** Children are ready for nonfiction *now*. As early as preschool or kindergarten, they read words such as *tyrannosaurus* and *Disneyland* when it matters to them. Start early to connect readers to their world, and they learn words meaningfully. Prepare students as nonfiction learners by building strong vocabularies and background knowledge.

Common Core State Standards

According to the Common Core State Standards (CCSS) adopted by forty-five states and three territories, from the earliest grades, we should introduce informational text. We need to increasingly emphasize reading and understanding informational text. As early childhood educators, we prepare students by introducing specialized vocabulary and informational texts in our reading.

The chart below shows how the adventures in chapters 2–8 correlate to the Common Core State Standards.

READING STANDARDS FOR INFORMATIONAL TEXT

KEY IDEAS AND DETAILS

1. Grade K: With prompting and support, ask and answer questions about key details in a text.	**CHAPTERS 2–8**
Grade 1: Ask and answer questions about key details in a text.	**CHAPTERS 2–8**
2. Grade K: With prompting and support, identify the main topic and retell key details of a text.	**CHAPTERS 2, 4–8**
Grade 1: Identify the main topic and retell key details of a text.	**CHAPTERS 2–8**
3. Grade K: With prompting and support, describe the connection between two individuals, events, ideas, or pieces of information in a text.	**CHAPTERS 2–8**
Grade 1: Describe the connection between two individuals, events, ideas, or pieces of information in a text.	**CHAPTERS 2–6, 8**

CRAFT AND STRUCTURE

4. Grade K: With prompting and support, ask and answer questions about unknown words in a text.	**CHAPTERS 2–8**
Grade 1: Ask and answer questions to help determine or clarify the meaning of words and phrases in a text.	**CHAPTERS 3–8**
5. Grade K: Identify the front cover, back cover, and title page of a book.	**CHAPTERS 3, 4, 6, 7**
Grade 1: Know and use various text features (e.g., headings, tables of contents, glossaries, electronic menus, icons) to locate key facts or information in a text.	**CHAPTERS 3–6, 8**
6. Grade K: Name the author and illustrator of a text and define the roles of each in presenting the ideas or information in a text.	**CHAPTERS 2–8**
Grade 1: Distinguish between information provided by pictures and other illustrations and information provided by the words in a text.	**CHAPTERS 2–8**

Teaching Real-Life Nonfiction Reading Skills in the K–1 Classroom © 2013 by Barbara S. Pinto • Scholastic Teaching Resources

INTEGRATION OF KNOWLEDGE AND IDEAS

7. Grade K:	With prompting and support, describe the relationship between illustrations and the text in which they appear (e.g., what person, place, thing, or idea in the text an illustration depicts).	**CHAPTERS 3–8**
Grade 1:	Use the illustrations and details in a text to describe its key ideas.	**CHAPTERS 3–8**
8. Grade K:	With prompting and support, identify the reasons an author gives to support points in a text.	**CHAPTERS 2–6, 8**
Grade 1:	Identify the reasons an author gives to support points in a text.	**CHAPTERS 3, 4, 6–8**
9. Grade K:	With prompting and support, identify basic similarities and differences between two texts on the same topic (e.g., in illustrations, descriptions, or procedures).	**CHAPTERS 4–8**
Grade 1:	Identify basic similarities in and differences between two texts on the same topic (e.g., in illustrations, descriptions, or procedures).	**CHAPTERS 4–8**

RANGE OF READING AND LEVEL OF TEXT COMPLEXITY

10. Grade K:	Actively engage in group reading activities with purpose and understanding.	**CHAPTERS 2, 4–8**
Grade 1:	With prompting and support, read informational texts appropriately complex for grade 1.	**CHAPTERS 3–8**

How to Use This Book

This book delivers seven authentic, practical adventures that connect the classroom with the outside world. It fosters an understanding of nonfiction skills and strategies through content-based adventures. Each adventure is fun and sets a purpose for reading. Whether you're sorting snacks or making lemonade, your students will be engaged while you cover a rich reading curriculum. As you proceed through the adventures, you'll be guided through the process of incorporating nonfiction skills appropriate to each adventure. Students develop the habits of mind necessary for nonfiction reading even before they open their reading books.

Teaching Real-Life Nonfiction Reading Skills in the K–1 Classroom presents *what* to teach in nonfiction and *why* it works, and shows you, step by step, *how to* do it. Students are curious, and they want to learn!

Chapter 1 explains what comprises nonfiction reading and why we teach it. Essential skills are listed with prompts.

In each of chapters 2–8, an authentic adventure is presented from start to finish, along with the corresponding nonfiction reading skills. Clear pacing, the necessary books and materials, step-by-step directions, a writing connection, and follow-up activities are built into each adventure.

The adventures are designed to carry instruction across the school year, so they can be done sequentially, but feel free to change the order to serve your corresponding units of study. Each adventure unfolds during a generous two- to four-week period, though this may be condensed. You may find that you move through them more quickly.

Use these adventures to enhance your phonics reading work and independent reading time by providing students with countless real reading opportunities and pave the path for them to read nonfiction informational texts.

Children learn from real-life adventures. Like a space journey, each reading adventure takes you and your students from the earthly comfort zone of the classroom to explore new, celestial territories. This expansion provides excitement, fueling new learning. We return "home" to reflect and consolidate new content using nonfiction strategies.

Each adventure consists of the five main sections described below. Suggestions for pacing are included throughout each adventure.

1. **Counting the Days (materials and preparation):** Every adventure requires preparation. Consider this section your itinerary: what to pack and where to go each day. You'll find a list of materials, book recommendations (a nonfiction and a fiction read-aloud selection), and preparation reminders.

2. **Fueling Up! Activities to keep you going:** On a space journey, you need to have fuel, proper clothing, and equipment. This section features activities that support learning, such as ongoing reading or learning centers. These activities accompany the main event and enhance the learning.

3. **Fasten Your Seat Belts! Ready to launch:** This section provides specific ways to launch the flight, such as brainstorming and reading aloud. A feature called "What This Sounds Like" in this and other sections offers a sample model of teacher dialogue.

4. **Lift Off! Begin the adventure:** This section includes a full, sequential description of each adventure.

5. **Back to Earth! Integrate the experience:** A writing connection plus other valuable learning extensions help integrate the adventure.

Each adventure begins with charts that show which nonfiction skills and strategies are emphasized in it:

- *Nonfiction Skills for This Adventure:* The broad skills targeted appear at the beginning of each chapter.

- *Spotlight on Nonfiction Strategies:* As the adventure proceeds, different nonfiction strategies are addressed in each main section.

Each chapter also contains the following sections:

- *Quick Look:* This overview chart shows the plan for the adventure, the reading work, writing connection, learning extensions, key concepts for content-area study, and pacing.

- *Successful Differentiation:* Steps for modification to guide learners at different levels appear here: "Supports" help simplify the tasks, while "Challenges" provide enrichment. Use them as needed for individual students.

- *Check in to Evaluate:* These focused questions help you assess learning.

- *Home-School Connection:* To build family involvement, this section offers tips and an explanation of parent letters.

- *Reproducibles:* Resources include a parent letter tailored for each adventure and other templates to save you time.

Finally, the Appendix contains references and additional resources.

■ Teaching Through Centers or Stations

The reading adventures in this book lend themselves to creative follow-up in center or station teaching. Modify both purpose and materials to create stations for "choice time" in the following specialized ways:

✔ Chapter 2

Words Live All Around Us: Word Hunt Walk: Word station with alphabet letters, signs, markers, pens, and books with environmental print

✔ Chapter 3

Words Keep Us Healthy: Sort Healthy Snacks: Restaurant station with utensils, placemats, sample menus, and blank paper to create menus

✔ Chapter 4

Words Inform Us About Our World: Create a School Newsletter: Newsletter station with templates, pens, scissors, magazines, and newspapers

✔ Chapter 5

Symbols Guide Us in New Places: Use a Map on a School or Neighborhood Treasure Hunt: Map center with maps, highlighter pens, and atlases

✔ Chapter 6

Words Help Us Make Choices: Plant a Salad: Plant center with seeds, pots, soil, books, small trowels, and photographs of plants

✔ Chapter 7

Words Teach Us, Step by Step: Make Lemonade: How-to center with instructions and materials for projects and how-to books

✔ Chapter 8

Words Inspire Celebrations: Investigate Invitations: Invitation station with sample commercial invitations (extend to thank-you and get-well cards), markers, templates, magazines, and glue

Everything you need to undertake authentic and engaging lessons to teach your students nonfiction reading skills, from start to finish, is at your fingertips. I hope you and your students enjoy the adventures in *Teaching Real-Life Nonfiction Reading Skills in the K–1 Classroom*!

Teaching Nonfiction Reading and Writing

Why Teach Nonfiction in the K–1 Classroom?

Nonfiction reading is real-life reading. We know that toddlers find countless things in the world fascinating: bugs and worms, how water pours, and what makes clouds, to name a few. This is the nonfiction of childhood.

Nonfiction reading is essential for our youngest learners. In their research, Duke and Bennett-Armistead (2003) have identified six key factors that support teaching nonfiction in the primary grades. These factors are inherent in the reading adventures in this book.

1. **Informational text is key to success in later schooling.** As the Common Core State Standards require more informational reading and as more nonfiction is available in print and on the Internet, our students' academic achievement increasingly depends on their ability to read this kind of text.

   Teachers help students build content literacy (using skills and strategies to read in a content area) and visual literacy (reading texts are organized by different structures, such as cause and effect) (Duke, 2003; Fountas & Pinnell, 2001; Blachowicz & Ogle, 2001). As children read graphics and pictures to understand the information in these texts, they learn to navigate the following visual features:

PRINT	GRAPHICS	ORGANIZATIONAL
Font	Diagrams	Table of contents
Bullets	Sketches	Glossary
Bold print	Maps	Index
Colored print	Photographs	Appendix
Italics	Zoom-in boxes	Pronunciation guide
Headings and subheadings		
Labels and captions		
Facts boxes		

2. **Informational text is ubiquitous in society.** An eight-year-old I tutored had two computers and an iPod. He would look up words by googling them! Nowadays, our youngsters are spending increasing amounts of time searching the Internet and reading

more informational text than even five years ago (Cohen & Cowan, 2008). However, even 30 years ago, the majority of adults' reading and writing was nonfiction (Venezky, 1982). The everyday adventures in this book guide children to evaluate and use information, and learn skills that help them apply what they know to their reading.

3. **Informational text is the preferred reading material for some children.** I used to wait until January to bring out my nonfiction books, thinking they were too hard for first graders earlier in the year. To my surprise, when children saw nonfiction books, the classroom tone changed. They hooted and clamored like kids lining up at an ice cream truck, but this time it was for their favorite topics, not ice cream! They pored over the books—almost inhaling the photographs and diagrams. When teachers introduce nonfiction in the fall, many reluctant readers are thrilled! Statistics show that older students often prefer reading nonfiction, especially boys and remedial students (Monson, 2012). In my experience, it's true for younger students, too.

4. **Informational text often addresses children's interests and questions.** Children are curious and have strong interests from a young age. Perhaps you know kindergarten students like George, a train enthusiast who could name every type of train car, or Cameron, our Civil War aficionado who learned accurate details of battles from his grandfather. These children remind us that passion leads to learning. Every day young children ask questions such as "Why does it snow?" Although it can be daunting to answer some questions, I am encouraged by my students' deep thirst for information. We quench that thirst by offering informational texts and rich activities.

5. **Informational text builds knowledge of the natural and social world.** Recently, while reading a story about getting lost at a mall, some students of mine became confused. They had never seen a mall, which is a hard concept for city kids. Experience prepares students for more effective reading; lack of experience may be a deficit. We can expose children to a range of experiences to support their reading.

   Yet direct exposure is not always possible (no field trip to the mall)! This lack of experience can be counteracted with extensive reading and listening, which can develop students' knowledge of the world (Anderson & Guthrie, 1999; Duke & Kays, 1998; Wilson & Anderson, 1986).

6. **Informational text may help build vocabulary and other kinds of literacy knowledge.** After making lemonade as a class, many of my students started using new words. I heard Tracy say she was "boiling," and Tommy said his partner "squeezed" his hand. Clearly, the activity influenced their vocabulary. In nonfiction work, we focus more on vocabulary and language development than in fiction (Mason, Peterman, Powell, & Kerr, 1989; Pellegrini, Perlmutter, Galda, & Brody, 1990). There are benefits to presenting activities and tying them into reading and writing (Bortnem, 2008).

■ What Do We Mean by Nonfiction Reading?

Definitions of nonfiction may vary somewhat, but we can agree that this type of text conveys information about the natural or social world and is an important part of inquiry-based learning (Duke, 2003; Flowers & Flowers, 2009). Informational text is organized by topic and supporting details, as opposed to literary text, which follows a narrative structure for a story, poem, or drama.

I define nonfiction as factual texts, which include informational and procedural texts. In this book, most of the chapters focus on informational texts, whereas Chapter 7, "Words Teach Us, Step by Step: Make Lemonade," is a journey in following procedural directions.

 BREAKDOWN OF NONFICTION SKILLS AND STRATEGIES

Classroom Application of Key Nonfiction Reading Skills and Strategies

Listed below you'll find nonfiction skills to teach and strategies to use. These skills develop like muscles. The more you use them, the stronger they get. Under each skill are multiple strategies, in parentheses, explained with prompts and questions for you to use. As students apply strategies, they build and strengthen these necessary skills.

■ Skill: Generate and Apply Background Knowledge

Gather baskets of related books for each study, along with read-aloud selections. Before launching the adventure, assess students' prior understanding by listening to discussions as they browse books and talk with their partners during read-aloud. As you listen, note the language students use, what they know, and what confuses them. Introduce related vocabulary in context.

- **Connect with a topic.** ("Did you ever do anything like this?" "Did you ever see a ____?")

- **Activate prior knowledge.** ("Remember when you saw ____ or did ____ or heard a book about ____?" "You already know something about this!")

- **Apply background knowledge to understand a text.** ("You know how to ____, so imagine what's happening here." "You've seen ____ like this before, so think about this." "If you know ____, then maybe ____.")

- **Predict based on prior knowledge.** ("Since we know about ____, we can think about what information we're going to learn." "Think about what you already know about ____. Might a ____ really do that?")

■ Skill: Understand Structure

Expose children to a diversity of books with various formats (e.g., all about, how-to, letter, Q&A). Be on the lookout for books that contain several formats; for example, a book about dogs, with a how-to on bathing a dog, or a book about a community that features a map. In addition to structure, explicit teaching of ways to read and understand different types of layouts helps students build confidence across books.

- **Notice print in varied places.** ("Do you see words in different places?" "Remember to look in every corner of the page to find information.")

- **Navigate through text features: read captions, headings, maps, diagrams, tables; learn from pictures and photographs.** ("Look at the ____ [feature] in the ____. This is a special way to show information.")

- **Navigate different layouts: e.g., boxes, print in different places.** ("Look at the picture and caption. How do they go together?" "Remember to read all the parts of the page.")

- **Read procedural text: follow a sequence.** ("This teaches you how to ____. What materials do you need?" "It's important to do this in an exact order. Look at the number before each step. What does it teach you?")

- **Use text features (font, size, italics, bold print) as cues.** ("Notice how this looks. This is a clue that tells us ____." "Look at ____. When the words look this way [bold, italics], this means ____.")

■ Skill: Learn and Apply Vocabulary

Building vocabulary is a vital nonfiction skill for content learning. To help children retain words, keep visual reminders of new vocabulary (e.g., word walls and charts) and encourage them to use those words in conversation. Student-created books provide a source for rereading and reinforcement. Students learn that specialized words in books need to be figured out. Glossaries can also help.

- **Acquire nonfiction-specialized vocabulary.** ("This word means ____. It goes with the topic of ____.")

- **Generate new vocabulary.** ("What would you call ____?" "Do you know a word that means the same as ____?")

- **Understand vocabulary in context.** ("What could this word mean in this sentence? Think of what you're learning and picture it." "What other word means the same thing?")

- **Build content knowledge base.** ("You know a few things about ____ now. Let's review them." "What more do you think we can learn?" "What words remind you of this topic?")

- **Use a glossary.** ("There's a special part of the book that tells you what these boldface words mean. Look there for help.")

■ Skill: Group Information

Grouping information leads to better understanding. Provide sorting opportunities with everyday objects. Children can sort objects into groups based on various features (e.g. color, texture, use). Then they name what belongs in a group, as well as what would not belong. The language children use in everyday sorting activities carries over to content-related sorting as well as to categorizing when they read nonfiction.

- **Understand dominant features of a group.** ("How are these two alike? What is the same about them?")

- **Generalize information.** ("If ____ and ____ go together, what can you say about both of them?")

- **Compare and contrast.** ("How is ____ the same as ____? How are they different?")

- **Classify: sort into groups based on dominant features.** ("Which go together? Why?" "Which fits this group? Which does not fit?")

- **Categorize information into groups: naming the groups.** ("How do these go together? What can we call them?" "What else belongs in this group?")

■ Skill: Deepen Understanding

As children become more proficient thinkers, they learn to apply these comprehension strategies across genres—from fiction to nonfiction. Provide models in big books and articles for better understanding. When reading aloud, stop and model the skills below. Point out headings and photographs that help children determine the importance of information, author's viewpoint, and main idea.

- **Question and comment.** ("What do you wonder about?" "You noticed ____. What does that make you think about?")

- **Figure out main idea(s) of a section or book.** ("What is this part/section/book mostly about?" "What is a big thing this book tries to teach us?")

- **Determine importance.** ("Is that a big topic or a little detail?" "What's most important here? What does the author write a lot about?")

- **Visualize what's happening.** ("Can you picture it?" "Close your eyes and picture what's happening.")

- **Find supporting details for evidence of critical thinking.** ("Can you look back and find parts that show or support ____?")

- **Infer the unknown from the known.** ("If you know ____, then what does that make you think?")

- **Determine author's purpose and point of view.** ("What do you think the author cares about?" "Think about a big thing the author wants you to know about.")

■ Skill: Research

Research at the primary level consists of learning how to find information by using different text features. Beginning research introduces students to skills in a light way. Use open-ended questions rather than yes-or-no questions (e.g., "What do birds eat?" rather than "Do birds eat worms?"). Support this work through whole-class read-alouds and in small groups.

- **Preview the text.** ("Look over the pages. What kind of information is in this book?" "Can this book help me?")

- **Skim for information.** ("We're looking to find out ____. Let's go quickly and find pictures or words that help.")

- **Use table of contents and index to find information.** ("There are special parts to help us find things. Let's see how they work." "What can you find out in the ____?")

- **Get information from pictures and photographs.** ("Can these details in the pictures help me find out ____? Let's look closely and see what we can learn.")

- **Find answers to questions.** ("What are you curious about? How can we use this book to figure it out?" "What features can help?")

- **Compare facts across texts.** ("In this book it says ____ about ____, but in that book it says ____. How is that the same or different?")

- **Organize information.** ("What can you find out about how a ____ lives? Can you find a few parts that are all about how a ____ lives?")

- **Connect facts to form a theory.** ("You found out ____ and ____ about ____. Let's think of a big idea that connects these." "If ____ and ____ are true, then what do you think would be a big idea about ____?")

These six skills are implicit in every adventure in this book. The chart below shows where skills are more *explicitly* taught in chapters 2–8.

SKILL	ADVENTURE						
	Chapter 2	Chapter 3	Chapter 4	Chapter 5	Chapter 6	Chapter 7	Chapter 8
Generate and Apply Background Knowledge	✔	✔	✔	✔	✔	✔	✔
Understand Structure	✔		✔	✔	✔	✔	
Learn and Apply Vocabulary	✔	✔	✔	✔		✔	✔
Group Information	✔	✔	✔	✔		✔	✔
Deepen Understanding		✔	✔		✔	✔	✔
Research			✔		✔	✔	✔

Teach Nonfiction: Instructional Strategies and Tips

Knowing what to teach is a great start. But I wouldn't be doing my job if I didn't impart some broad-based ways to get that knowledge across. What basic *instructional* strategies give you mileage during nonfiction reading workshop time? How do you start? How do you construct a meaningful reading time? What is the best way to navigate through the reading adventures in this book?

■ Instructional Strategies for Nonfiction Reading Time

ALLOW TIME FOR EXPLORATION OF BOOKS AND MATERIALS

- Allow choice according to students' interest.
- Emphasize information in illustrations.
- Allow multiple days for browsing.
- Compare books on the same topic.
- Expand the definition of reading sources (see the list at the right). Collect magazines, photographs (add writing on them!), food wrappers, advertisements, brochures, toddler books, Web site printouts, and any other related and informative sources.

ENCOURAGE STUDENT TALK (MODEL BEHAVIORS YOU WANT STUDENTS TO DEVELOP)

- Words and pictures are both sources of information:
  - Talk about pictures.
  - Point and name details.
  - Discuss meaning.
- Talk with a partner:
  - Teach children how to take turns.
- Talk in general ways about what is interesting:
  - I notice . . .
  - This is really cool because . . .

Sources of Informational Text in Daily Life

- *Concept books:* Concepts such as shapes, opposites, signs, and food are represented in these basic texts.
- *Environmental print:* Words in the world teach names for things and places—from the bus stop sign to the milk carton.
- *Media and print in the world:* Children are exposed to many forms of information, such as movie posters and articles in children's magazines and newspapers.
- *Web sites, blogs, and online newsletters:* Internet sources are increasingly popular sources for information.
- *Brochures and pamphlets:* At the zoo and other cultural spots, plaques and signs teach about the places they represent.
- *Literary nonfiction:* Stories may contain nonfiction content. Though they have plots and characters, we learn facts from books, such as *Snail's Spell* by Joanna Ryder and *Stellaluna* by Janell Cannon.

- Use prompts to encourage discussion. Students rely on pictures to start conversation:

  I see _____ (a bird on a tree). So I can learn that _____ (birds climb or fly).

  So I think _____ (birds like to be in trees).

  And I wonder _____ (where else do birds go)?

- Use simple notations on sticky notes to create a place to stop and talk:

  - **?** Something I wonder about

  - **!** A surprising fact or idea

  - **F** A new fact

  - **✓** Something I like

- Compare sources; use differences to dig deeper and think:

  This book says _____.

  But this book says _____.

  That makes me think _____ because _____ .

MODEL BY THINKING ALOUD

- Explicitly name what you model.

- Use big books and read-alouds to teach nonfiction strategies.

USE GENRE-SPECIFIC LANGUAGE TO DIFFERENTIATE FICTION FROM NONFICTION

- **Fiction:** When talking about a story, book, or passage, I ask, "What is this about?" "What just happened?" or "Tell me about the story."

- **Nonfiction:** When talking about a nonfiction essay, text, or passage, I ask, "What can you learn?" "What did this teach you?" or "Tell me about the information in this text."

ALLOW A BUZZ IN THE ROOM: READING VOICES

Some teachers desire complete silence during reading time, yet very young children need to read in low voices (subvocalization). Student discussions about nonfiction include description and questions. Divide your workshop time: let partners talk first, then read independently in whisper voices. Flip back and forth to extend reading time, and listen to the buzz about books!

Teaching Real-Life Nonfiction Reading Skills in the K–1 Classroom © 2013 by Barbara S. Pinto • Scholastic Teaching Resources

■ Tips for Navigating Through These Reading Adventures

BE PREPARED

- **Know which materials you need and when you need them:** Check the "Counting the Days" section in the beginning of the chapter. Modify each adventure according to time and interest. Locate the ready-made reproducibles at the end of the chapter.

- **Books are wonderful resources; organize them:** Gather the books you will need before each adventure. Set them out in the following ways:

  - *Table baskets:* Create baskets of books for each table for independent browsing. Place five to ten books in each basket. Rotate the baskets daily.

  - *Read-aloud basket:* After reading aloud topic-related books, put them in a large basket in the classroom library or another prominent place. Provide a time for students to reread these familiar books (e.g., snack time, choice time, after unpacking, or between activities).

  - *Student input:* Invite children to add books to the table baskets, either from home or the library. Encourage the addition of related materials such as magazines and brochures.

  - *Find the right books:* Though this may initially seem challenging, much of this work is done for you; this book provides suggestions of wonderful titles for each adventure. Supplement these suggestions with appropriate choices already in your rooms, using the following criteria:

    * Match the reading level of your class or go slightly below it.

    * Match the nonfiction skills, strategies, and features in each adventure.

    * Find books containing both familiar and new content.

    * Find big books and regular-size books with large, realistic pictures and photographs.

    * Find books your students can easily read in one or two sittings.

    * Find engaging and entertaining texts.

    * Choose texts you enjoy reading *and* rereading.

- **Prepare stopping points when you read aloud:** Before each reading, I choose pages to stop at to stimulate partner conversation. I put a sticky note with a leading question, using the teaching focus to help. Each chapter has one read-aloud selection already laid out for you.

- **Keep a balanced read-aloud diet:** Read both fiction and nonfiction all year long to your students. Many teachers, myself included, tend to favor fiction for reading aloud. (True confession: When I first compiled read-aloud texts for this book, they were mostly fiction, too!). In this book I describe either the fiction selection or the nonfiction selection. While I read both selections to my class, here I've chosen the book that creates more anticipation and connects to the purpose of the adventure. Sometimes a fiction selection is more motivating as a launch for a study. Through fiction, readers can also learn about the real world. Researchers have noted an overwhelming predilection for fiction in early childhood classrooms. And while that may be true, let's not ignore nonfiction! From the first week of school to the hazy days of June, readers need to hear the sound of, and see the structure of, informational texts as an ordinary, not an extraordinary, event!

DIFFERENTIATE

Teachers know that not every student is ready for every task, so we adjust the learning to match the learner. There are times when students need modifications for success. Each chapter provides suggestions for differentiation. Differentiation may be based on academic need or interest. Consider grouping differently (partners, collaborative groups) and adjusting the process or product.

ASSESS AS YOU GO

Observe student behavior, vocabulary, and engagement. Each "Back to Earth!" section contains a special part called "Check in to Evaluate," which provides key questions to assess students' comprehension of content and their understanding of the characteristics of nonfiction.

KEEP IT FUN!

I have always instinctively known that good teaching involves fun. Now I have solid research to back up my intuition. Learning occurs in "aha" moments and an atmosphere of discovery. Fun equals engagement and investment (Willis, 2006; Slade, 2010).

I agree—fun is essential! The adventures in this book are crafted activities, opportunities to teach nonfiction skills and strategies in a memorable way. (Some people say I've never grown up, and it's probably true—I want my classes to be festive and fun!) I chose to teach the youngest grades to be with spirited children, who are playful by nature. Good teaching provides them with cherished activities that are learning-rich and joyful. It's like fertilizing the soil with plant food and nutrients, then planting seeds to create beautiful flower beds!

Each of the following chapters contains a reading adventure, self-contained and ready to be replicated. They are the *how* of teaching nonfiction. Enjoy the journey of nonfiction and content-area reading.

Words Live All Around Us: Word Hunt Walk

Children learn how to classify information as word detectives.

A Quick Look at Chapter 2

THE ADVENTURE	Take a learning walk to find words (environmental print) on signs.
READING WORK	Read signs. Reread these words on a specialized word wall. Read our homemade big book. Read small copies of our big book.
WRITING CONNECTION	Write a class big book about signs found on the Word Hunt Walk.
LEARNING EXTENSIONS	Have children "read the room." Add place signs to familiar big books. Set up an environmental word wall.
CONTENT-AREA WORK	Key Concepts of an Environmental Study: • What kind of print is in our environment? • Which words do we use to find places? • How do signs and words in our school help us?
PACING	11–12 days

Nonfiction Skills for This Adventure

- **Generate and Apply Background Knowledge**
- **Understand Structure**
- **Learn and Apply Vocabulary**
- **Group Information**

Why Are We Doing This?

Was I surprised when Matt, my three-year-old, pointed and read the park sign, "Keep off the gwass"! He had seen and heard it dozens of times on our daily jaunt. Now Matt was so aware of the sign that he was reading it and knew its purpose!

Signs tell us what to do and help us find places. Skillful adults draw children's attention to signs they see daily. At school, teachers play a leading role in raising children's awareness of print in their environment, as we'll do on this learning walk. In this adventure, students play word detectives as they hunt, locate, classify, and categorize the words they find around them, thereby developing curiosity for words. Watch your little researchers, clipboard and pencil ready, point at each new word and discover the magic of print! They will begin to decipher these squiggles and learn about the world around them.

 COUNTING THE DAYS

What you need

MATERIALS

✔ Books:

- Fiction read-aloud selection: *Night at the Fair* by Donald Crews

- Nonfiction read-aloud selection: *I Read Signs* by Tana Hoban

- Other related literature: Look for books that show the relevance of signs and have text in pictures, such as the following:

    Signs in Our World by John Searcy

    The Signmaker's Assistant by Tedd Arnold

    City Signs by Zoran Milich

    Signs by David Bauer

✔ Reproducibles:

- Parent Letter, p. 35 (1 copy for each family)
- Word Hunt Walk Recording Sheet, p. 36 (1 copy for each child)
- Detective Spyglass, p. 37 (1 copy for each child)

Plan for Spontaneity!

Proficient teachers plan, plan, plan and then act surprised, as if the signs suddenly appeared! For example, this is how a master teacher introduced his lesson: "You know, I just had a good idea! Let's write letters to my friend in California with our ideas!" His "good idea" was far from spontaneous; it was a prepared, seemingly casual introduction. A student teacher who was watching later commented, "He never does any planning!" not realizing that good teachers build motivation and enthusiasm by appearing to think out loud. Likewise, when I find a sign on the walk, I exclaim, "Oh my, look here! I just found a word. What does it say? What's in this place?" Here's our chance to be theatrical and to act amazed by the words that children find around us!

✔ Other Materials:

- clipboards (1 for each child)
- sentence strips or blank flash cards (for labeling the room)
- index cards and metal loose-leaf ring
- chart paper and marker or pocket chart and cardstock cards
- easel
- scissors
- sticky notes
- camera
- art materials, such as colored pencils, crayons, and paints
- optional: a copy of the song "Going on a Word Hunt"

PREPARATION

✔ 1 week before:

- *Prepare stopping points in the literature: Notice the importance of signs and words in the text of* Night at the Fair. *Flag places to stop that help students think about how signs help us navigate. Choose signs such as "Tickets" and those that identify where to eat and where to find prizes. Flag the signs in* I Read Signs *that appear in your environment.*

- *Familiarize students with the school by taking a general walk and naming places you see.*

- *On your own, take a pre-walk to map out your school Word Hunt Walk route: Notice where signs exist and where they are needed. Make a list of places to visit, signs to notice, and signs to create.*

- *Take photographs of signs at your school and save them for later use.*

- *Optional: Chart the song "Going on a Word Hunt" and introduce it to the class.*

  GOING ON A WORD HUNT (sing to the tune of "Going on a Bear Hunt")

  We're going on a word hunt!
  We're going on a word hunt!
  We're gonna find a big one!
  We're gonna find a big one!
  I'm not afraid!
  I'm not afraid!
  Are you?
  Are you?
  Not me!
  Not me!

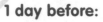 **1 day before:**

- *Set out chart paper or a pocket chart.*
- *Copy the Parent Letter reproducible to send home after the Word Hunt Walk.*
- *Place a copy of the Word Hunt Walk Recording Sheet on a clipboard for each child.*
- *Cut out a spyglass on the Detective Spyglass reproducible for each child.*

 FUELING UP! (ONGOING)

Activities to keep you going

Infuse content into daily discussions. Before and after the school Word Hunt Walk, start noticing words on T-shirts, backpacks, and so on—wherever they appear in the school environment.

Inform students about jobs and places at school. Create a chart that lists school jobs and where they take place, as shown below.

Spotlight on Nonfiction Strategies

✳ Predict based on prior knowledge
✳ Generate new vocabulary
✳ Understand vocabulary in context

JOB	PLACE
secretary	office
teacher	art room
cook	cafeteria
custodian	halls

Ready to launch

This section builds on what children already know and helps them find out more about their school and signs around them.

■ Set a Real-Life Purpose (1 day)

The day before the adventure, introduce the idea by sharing an analogy or a quick story. This is an effective way to illustrate the real-life uses of a skill.

WHAT THIS SOUNDS LIKE

After the summer, I came into school and learned that the nurse's office had moved. I didn't know where to find it! So you know what I did? I walked around and looked at the signs on the doors until I found a sign that read "Nurse."

Reading signs in our environment helps us find places. Tomorrow, we're going to explore our school by going on a Word Hunt Walk! We're going to be word detectives and look for signs that tell us the names of locations or places. I even have some detective spyglasses for you to use! (Distribute a Detective Spyglass to each student.)

■ Brainstorm Place Signs (same day)

Then ask students to think about the places they'll see on your walk. Record their suggestions on chart paper or on cardstock cards for a pocket chart. Also, copy these words on index cards and attach them to a metal loose-leaf ring so you can take them on the walk tomorrow. Listen for how well children discriminate between a place and people or things, and lead them to discriminate between place names and other signs.

WHAT THIS SOUNDS LIKE

Before we go on our Word Hunt Walk tomorrow, let's predict what place names we think we'll find. When we predict, we make a guess about something. Who thinks they know a sign we might see? Remember, not all signs name a place. On our Word Hunt Walk, we want to look for places. (Record predictions.) *Here's a song about going on a hunt.* (Display *"Going on a Word Hunt."*) *We can sing it tomorrow. Let's practice.*

Possible Prompts:

• *Does anyone have brothers or sisters in school? Do you know the name of their teachers? We might see classrooms labeled with teachers' names!*

• *Does anyone belong to an after-school club? Do you know the name of the room or the place where the club is held?*

- *Think about how we walk to our classroom each day. What places do we pass? Do you remember if any of those places has a sign?*
- *Think about our special classes. Do you think those classrooms or spaces might have signs to help people find them?*

Tips

✔ Accept all predictions, even if you know that the place does not have a sign.

✔ Ask questions to make sure children understand the place: Parents work in this place. What do you think they do for the school?

■ Read Aloud to Explore Place Names (2 days)

FICTION READ-ALOUD: *NIGHT AT THE FAIR* (1 DAY)

Often the read-aloud is the launch of a study. But here I wanted to present it right before the actual walk. This can even be done on the same day if your schedule allows. Emphasize environmental print by noticing signs in the illustrations and explaining vocabulary. Point out how signs identify places.

Before reading: Explain that sometimes print occurs in illustrations.

During reading: Invite children to explore key pages and note what appears in illustrations.

After reading: Ask children to talk to partners about an important sign in the book.

WHAT THIS SOUNDS LIKE

Before reading: Today, we're going to read a book called Night at the Fair. *I want you to look closely at the pictures in this book. You'll notice that there are signs with words in the illustrations. These are place names, just like the place names we'll hunt for in school. Now, as we read, notice what words you see and think about the place at the fair. Are all signs place names? Put your thumb up if you see a word in the pictures. Let's read it and decide if it's a place name.*

During reading: Let's take a close look at this page. Look at the place shown on the page: "Tickets." Can you imagine what happens there? When would you be at a ticket booth? Think about this place and what happens there.

After reading: Now turn to a partner. Talk about one sign that you think is important. What do you think would happen if there were no sign there? Can you imagine another place at the fair? What would the sign for that place read?

NONFICTION READ-ALOUD: *I READ SIGNS* (1 DAY)

This book features vivid photographs of actual street signs and includes a full list of the signs at the end. Read it and ask students to notice signs in the neighborhood near school. Talk about which signs show a place. A good time to read this would be after the walk itself or choose another day to share it.

■ Label the Classroom to Classify Places (1–2 days)

Day 1: Connect your read-aloud discussion to labeling classroom places. Invite children to create labels for important classroom places. During this process, discuss categorizing information. The goal is to label place names, not materials; for example, instead of labeling counting bears in the math center, help students understand that the bears are materials. The math center is the place that you want to label. (Select a few children to put up signs written on blank flash cards or sentence strips.)

Day 2: On chart paper, start a list of name places versus things in your classroom to help children see the difference between the two. (See the sample below.)

Label a place in the classroom.

WHAT THIS SOUNDS LIKE

Day 1: *When we read* Night at the Fair, *we discovered how important signs are. I notice that we don't have very many signs in our classroom! It would be useful to make signs to label important places in our room, so visitors can easily find them. What are some places in our room we could label?*

Day 2: *Let's think of a place in our room, such as the math center. Look at the chart. It goes under the word* Place *on our chart. What are some things we'd find in the math center? Yes, we have rulers there. I'll write that down under the word* Thing. *Do you see the difference between a place and a thing?*

PLACE	THING
Library	Books
Math center	Rulers
Sink area	Soap
Meeting area	Rug
Block corner	Blocks

Classroom Application: One child's understanding

"Can I put a sign on a book?" Peter asked. I responded that we were looking for *places* in our room. "Is a book a place?" I asked. Peter realized that the book belonged in a basket in the library and that "library" was the *place* where books go. I explained to Peter that when we sort things, we call a book a *thing,* and library is where the book goes, or a *place.*

A question such as this helps children categorize names of things versus names of places.

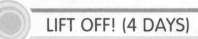

Begin the adventure

Even five-year-old detectives notice what's around them and can sort out information that is useful to them.

■ Set Out on the Word Hunt Walk

Before setting out on the walk, read through the list of places you predicted you'd see with the class. Take along these word cards on a metal ring. The word hunt is in two parts: First, you'll engage students in looking for existing signs, then take a day or so to put up signs that are needed. Make sure each child has a detective spyglass to use while searching for signs. Distribute clipboards with Word Hunt Walk Recording Sheets and discuss where you might look for words around school. Guide children to understand that signs are most likely to appear on doors and walls and that they may be high on a wall, such as an exit sign, or above a door. They will use the word cards to find signs and read them as they go.

Days 1–2: Noticing existing signs

During the walk, stop at the places named on the word cards and other key locations that have signs. Make sure to name the word and explain the meaning, so new vocabulary is built. Match your word card with the sign, comparing the letters one by one. Split the walk into two days by doing either one floor at a time or one part of the building each day. Aim for two consecutive days if possible. Remember to visit prime locations such as the gym, yard, and auditorium.

Have children record the words on the Word Hunt Walk Recording Sheet. Encourage them to write or draw as much as possible without getting frustrated. Discuss the function of each place and why it's important. Compare which signs are places and which are not. Help children to understand the feature that makes something a *place*.

WHAT THIS SOUNDS LIKE

Prior to walk: *Okay, today is our big day! We're going on a Word Hunt Walk! Remember, we'll be searching for signs that name important places in our school. Let's reread the list of places we're going to visit.* (Reread the list on the chart paper or in the pocket chart.) *Here's a clipboard, pencil, and a Word Hunt Walk Recording Sheet for each of you. And don't forget your detective spyglasses! We'll stop at important places and look for signs. Remember, a place is where something is. For example, on our way to Art, we pass some of the places that are important in our school, such as the lunchroom. We'll stop at each place to remind ourselves why it's important and who works there.*

Spotlight on Nonfiction Strategies

* Predict based on prior knowledge
* Generate new vocabulary
* Understand vocabulary in context
* Understand dominant features of a group
* Compare and contrast

On the walk: *Look, here's the office. It is called the main office because it is so important. Do you know some of the things that happen at the main office? Did you ever bring our attendance folder here? That's because the secretaries who work in the main office collect information.*

When you see a sign, we'll read it and find out if it names a place. Then we'll write the name down or draw a picture on our recording sheet as best we can. That way, we'll remember the places we visited.

Possible Prompts:

- *Is this a place?*
- *Where is the sign? Let's read it.* (Provide a sentence with the word in it.)
- *Say the word. This means ____.*
- *Who works here?*
- *What do they do?*

Days 3–4: Notice where signs are missing

On a separate day, walk along the same route and this time notice where signs *could* be. Keep a list of students' responses. When you return to the classroom later that day (or the next day), invite children to create signs for these places using blank flash cards. After getting permission, hang the signs around the school. If time allows, take a follow-up walk to hang the signs.

WHAT THIS SOUNDS LIKE

Remember how we found places at school? A place is where something happens. Today, we're going to look for places where there are no signs! I'll keep a list of the places that need signs. Then we'll return to the classroom and make those signs.

Possible Prompts:

- *What is this place?*
- *Where is the sign? Can we make one?*

Integrate the experience

Continue to look for places where you can put words in your classroom and around school. Point out how environmental print is used during daily travels. Help children retain words by frequent rereading and use in their writing.

■ WRITING CONNECTION: Make a Class big book (3 days)

Soon your students will surprise you by reading words such as *gymnasium* and *counselor's office* and understanding them in context!

Day 1: Generate sentences from the list of places for a class big book. Engage students in a discussion of their Word Hunt Walk and listen to patterns in their language structure; for example, are they saying, "I see . . . " or do they say, "I saw . . ." or "We visited . . ."? Consider the reading level of students and construct a book to match the language patterns in books they are reading, using a more or less predictable repetition. Write the sentences on chart paper for everyone to see, or a small chart tablet for students to illustrate later.

WHAT THIS SOUNDS LIKE

What can we say about the places we saw in our school? What would be a good way to tell others about our Word Hunt Walk and what we found? Tell your partner. (Listen to responses.) *Let's use the list we made before we went on our walk to write sentences about our word hunt. We'll name some of the places and draw pictures, too!*

A book made by early emergent readers might look like this:

[page 1] I see the gymnasium.

[page 2] I see the office.

[page 3] I see the yard.

[page 4] I see the jungle gym.

[page 5] I see the school!

One kindergarten teacher decided to write "We see . . ." as the repeating pattern since both *we* and *see* were newly introduced sight words. A first-grade class, practicing the words *our* and *has*, created the following text for its book:

We see signs!

[page 1] Our school has a gymnasium.

[page 2] Our school has an office.

[page 3] But best of all, our school has our class!

Day 2: Have children illustrate the pages of the big book or use photographs you took on the Word Hunt Walk.

Day 3: Type the text and duplicate it to create small copies of the classroom big book for book baskets. You can make a copy for each child or several for the classroom library. This provides reading material that students can use to review place words.

Reread the big book for shared reading as often as possible.

■ Learning Extension Activities (ongoing)

✔ Have children "read the room."

Use various charts and signs as a rich supply of familiar texts to reread. Select two to four children daily to have the honor of using your pointer during reading time as they reread print material.

As students develop as readers, their signs morph into phrases, then sentences. For instance, a sign that read "Math" changes to "Math Center" and later to "the Math Center" and finally to "Here is the Math Center." Students who are practicing one-to-one correspondence in reading can use the room signs to support their growing capacity to read print.

✔ Add place signs to familiar big books.

Select a classroom big book that does not contain environmental print (words in the illustrations). Use sticky notes to add signs to the illustrations. Refer to the mentor texts, *Night at the Fair* and *I Read Signs,* to remind students of how signs are useful.

✔ Set up an environmental word wall.

Assign a place in the room for a school or an environmental print word wall for reference. Add logos and familiar signs, such as the school logo and a stop sign. Read these often with students and encourage them to add to the wall.

■ Check in to Evaluate

1. Do students notice environmental print?

2. Can students name some places at school?

3. Can students distinguish between a place and a thing?

■ Home-School Connection

Though it is natural to make children aware of environmental print, this process may be unfamiliar to parents. It is important to remind parents that, even with their busy lives, there are little things they can do to make their children aware of words in their world.

The parent letter gives tips to promote awareness of print, reinforce vocabulary, and build conversation around print. Recommend the following activities when the opportunity arises:

- Play a game to find signs in the bus or in the playground.
- Have children copy signs they find near home.

■ Reproducibles

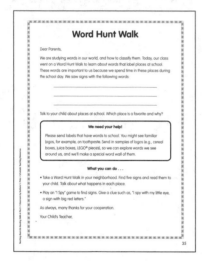

PARENT LETTER (This is a quick note to send home to parents after the Word Hunt Walk. Fill in the actual words that were found on your walk.)

WORD HUNT WALK RECORDING SHEET

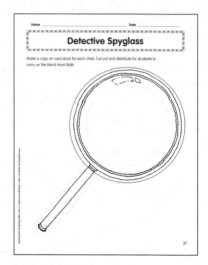

DETECTIVE SPYGLASS

Word Hunt Walk

Dear Parents,

We are studying words in our world, and how to classify them. Today, our class went on a Word Hunt Walk to learn about words that label places at school. These words are important to us because we spend time in these places during the school day. We saw signs with the following words:

_____

_____

_____

Talk to your child about places at school. Which place is a favorite and why?

We need your help!

Please send labels that have words to school. You might see familiar logos, for example, on toothpaste. Send in samples of logos (e.g., cereal boxes, juice boxes, LEGO® pieces), so we can explore words we see around us, and we'll make a special word wall of them.

What you can do . . .

• Take a Word Hunt Walk in your neighborhood. Find five signs and read them to your child. Talk about what happens in each place.

• Play an "I Spy" game to find signs. Give a clue such as, "I spy with my little eye, a sign with big red letters."

As always, many thanks for your cooperation.

Your Child's Teacher,

Word Hunt Walk Recording Sheet

At school, we found these places.

_____	_____
_____	_____
_____	_____

a b c d e f g h i j k l m n o p q r s t u v w x y z
A B C D E F G H I J K L M N O P Q R S T U V W X Y Z

Detective Spyglass

Make a copy on card stock for each child. Cut out and distribute for students to carry on the Word Hunt Walk.

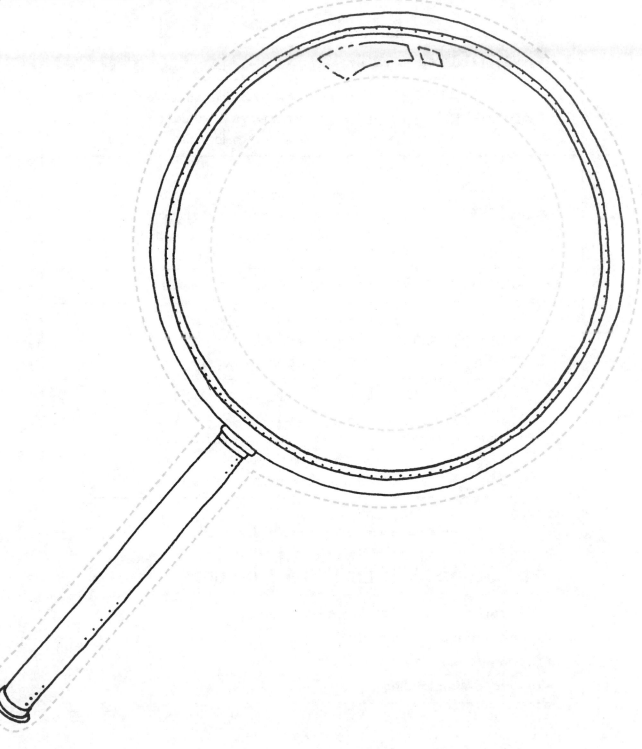

Chapter 3

Words Keep Us Healthy:
Sort Healthy Snacks

Children learn how to sort and classify, while learning about good nutrition.

A Quick Look at Chapter 3

THE ADVENTURE	Learn about the USDA food guide known as MyPlate. Sort food pictures by MyPlate food guide groups. Sort snacks by MyPlate food guide groups.
READING WORK	Read names of foods. Read books about nutrition and food. Read small student-authored books about snacks. Read informational magazines, such as *Scholastic News*.
WRITING CONNECTION	Write books about food for rereading.
LEARNING EXTENSIONS	Create Ideal Meal Placemats. Set up a restaurant center. Design food group collages.
CONTENT-AREA WORK	Key Concepts of a Nutrition Study: • What is the food guide? • What are the basic food groups? • Which foods belong in these groups? • What are examples of healthy choices?
PACING	15–18 days

Nonfiction Skills for This Adventure

- **Generate and Apply Background Knowledge**
- **Learn and Apply Vocabulary**
- **Group Information**
- **Deepen Understanding**

Why Are We Doing This?

One of my students, Henry, had a severe nut allergy. If he sat near a child eating a peanut granola bar, he could have an anaphylactic attack. After a serious talk about having a nut-free classroom, my students became guardians of their classmate, reading snack labels to protect him. Occasionally, they'd warn, "It's made near nuts!" My students checked all the ingredients on the labels; my job was to give them the tools to keep *themselves* safe.

Due to increased childhood obesity and diabetes, schools are taking more responsibility for instructing students about nutrition by promoting health fairs and creating alternative lunch options. The Sort Healthy Snacks adventure takes an important issue—safety and health—and makes it fun. Students examine snacks, group them based on the USDA food guide, and extend their learning in a number of ways. For example, by creating an Ideal Meal Placemat to use and share at home, children learn to sort and categorize in a natural way.

COUNTING THE DAYS

What you need

MATERIALS

✔ Books:

- Fiction read-aloud selection: *Sweet Tooth* by Margie Palatini
- Nonfiction read-aloud selection: *Good Enough to Eat: A Kid's Guide to Food and Nutrition* by Lizzy Rockwell
- Other related literature: Look for books that emphasize good nutrition and that engagingly present new information. These texts should inspire rather than preach. Here are some good examples:
  Gregory the Terrible Eater by Mitchell Sharmat and Jose Aruego
  Eating the Rainbow (Babies Everywhere) by Rena D. Grossman
  The Vegetables We Eat by Gail Gibbons

✔ Reproducibles:

- Parent Letter, p. 49 (1 copy for each family)
- Ideal Meal Placemat template, p. 50 (1 copy for each student)
- Food Picture Cards, p. 51 (1 copy for each pair and 1 copy for each reading basket)

✔ Other Materials:

- writing paper with a picture box and lines
- menu planning sheets available at supermarkets
- menus from neighborhood restaurants
- cardstock

- chart paper and marker
- sticky notes
- MyPlate USDA food guide (display copy and a smaller version for each reading basket) (www.choosemyplate.gov)
- baskets
- food-related articles from children's magazines
- pictures of food from adult and children's magazines
- scissors
- glue and tape
- clean, empty snack wrappers
- six large sheets of posterboard or easel paper
- materials for a restaurant center (menus, pretend and real snacks, placemats, utensils, dishes, napkins, order pads, play money, and so on)

PREPARATION

✔ 1 week before:

- *Prepare stopping points in the literature,* Sweet Tooth: *Flag places in the text where different sweet foods are named.*

- *Create a basket for each table with food-related reading material (books, articles, MyPlate food guide, Food Picture Cards, children's magazines)*

- *Collect snack food wrappers. Wash them out and save for sorting activity in the Lift Off! section.*

- *Collect pictures of food from adult and children's magazines.*

- *Copy the Parent Letter reproducible and send one home with each student.*

✔ 1 day before:

- *Copy the Ideal Meal Placemat (p. 50).*

- *Create two sets of food-group posters. For each set, write the name of a food group on a sheet of posterboard or easel paper: Fruits, Grains, Vegetables, Meat, and Dairy. Select a sample photo or illustration for each food group from magazines or Food Picture Cards and attach them to the corresponding posterboard.*

Activities to keep you going

Make sorting and nutrition common topics in your classroom.

Before and after the Sort Healthy Snacks adventure, infuse food vocabulary at snack time. Read snack labels and notice what children have for snacks. Point out when they have made good choices, without being judgmental. Be aware of good nutrition. Informally mention the names of food groups and specific foods to build vocabulary.

Sort materials in the math center to help students understand sorting. Create classroom sorting activities. Set up a routine for sorting and introduce related vocabulary (*sort, group, same, different, belongs together*). Display math materials and sort them. Name each sorted group by appropriate category.

Set up baskets of related materials: books, magazines, and food pictures about food and nutrition. Carve out a daily routine (10–15 minutes) for exploring reading baskets to help students learn food vocabulary and use it in context. Introduce a copy of the MyPlate food guide to help students learn about categorizing food and familiarize them with the Food Picture Cards. Collect children's magazines and newspapers to add to reading baskets. As students read, have them categorize food in the texts into food groups and also into groups of healthy versus unhealthy. Allow partners to talk about their choices.

Spotlight on Nonfiction Strategies

* Activate prior knowledge
* Generate vocabulary
* Understand vocabulary in context
* Build content knowledge base
* Classify and categorize

Ready to launch

■ Set a Real-Life Purpose (1 day)

A week before the adventure, post a display copy of the MyPlate food guide and talk about it. Explain how this food guide works and introduce the idea of learning about healthy eating.

WHAT THIS SOUNDS LIKE

This picture shows us how much of each kind of food is good for our bodies. It helps us remember how to eat in a healthy way. Let's read the names of the basic groups (fruits, vegetables, grains, protein, dairy). *The bigger sections of the plate show that you should eat more of that kind of food.*

Spotlight on Nonfiction Strategies

* Activate prior knowledge
* Generate vocabulary
* Build content knowledge base

- *Who can name one of the basic food groups?*
- *Which kind of food should we eat most? Which kind should we eat least?*

■ Create a Nutrition Word Wall (1 day)

Establish a place in the room to list new words for the study. Introduce one word (e.g., *nutrition*) and add one or two daily as the adventure continues. Frequently reread the words. As you do this, also review the categories on the food guide.

■ Read Aloud to Explore Food and Nutrition (3 days)

Use books to drive home the need for proper nutrition.

FICTION READ-ALOUD: *SWEET TOOTH* (2 DAYS)

As a prelude to the adventure, I introduce *Sweet Tooth*. In this romp, a demanding wisdom tooth dictates the main character's food choices, and ultimately readers come to understand the freedom of eating healthily. Talk about what happens when the main character, Stewart, eats too much sugar. Compare how the boy feels after eating all that sugar with how he'll feel when he eats healthy food.

Before reading: Guide children to think of healthy choices they already make. Discuss foods that they routinely eat. Ask children to imagine what would happen if they ate only sweets. Get them ready for the silly things in this story.

During reading: As the story progresses, have students think about the foods Stewart chooses. Ask them to name some of the sweet things he's eating.

After reading: Create a list of healthy and unhealthy foods. Ask children to think about how Stewart's behavior changed when he didn't eat sugar.

WHAT THIS SOUNDS LIKE

We are learning about the kinds of food that people need to stay healthy. So many of you already have such healthy snacks. I've noticed fruit and veggies such as carrots and celery. Some children have yogurt too! We are really taking care of our bodies. We want to learn more about good foods that help us to grow strong. I have two books that will help us learn more. The first one is so silly . . . you'll see!

Possible Prompts:
- *What are some good snack foods?*
- *What group do you think they belong to?*
- *Why do you have to be aware of what you eat?*

Before reading: What foods do you eat often? What do you think would happen if you only ate sweets? You'll hear about a boy who had a silly problem: His tooth makes him eat sweets. Think about what might happen if he keeps eating that way.

During reading: What sweet thing is Stewart eating now? Do you think he's making good choices? Let's see what happens next.

After reading: Think about which foods are healthy and which are unhealthy.

Possible Prompts:

- *I'm going to make a list, starting with candy. Under which heading should I write "candy"?*
- *Who can suggest another food? Which side should we put it on?*

On chart paper, create a two-column chart with the headings "Healthy" and "Unhealthy." Record students' responses.

HEALTHY FOODS	UNHEALTHY FOODS
cheese	candy

NONFICTION READ-ALOUD: *GOOD ENOUGH TO EAT: A KID'S GUIDE TO FOOD AND NUTRITION* **(1 DAY)**

Tell students that this book teaches about foods that make and keep a body healthy. Activate their prior knowledge by asking what they might find in a book about good things to eat. Generate a short list on chart paper. Add words to the chart of healthy and unhealthy foods you began in the fiction selection. Have children listen for healthy choices as you read.

LIFT OFF! (6–7 DAYS)

Begin the adventure

Make clear connections between children's experiences and new content. Food won't look the same again as students realize what's truly good for them.

■ Step 1: Use MyPlate food guide to introduce healthy eating (2 days)

For this adventure, I use stories from my own life to start children thinking. Use the display copy of the MyPlate food guide to show children that healthy eating matters. Give a copy of the Ideal Meal Placemat to each child. Point out that the plate on the placemat shows the food guide. Review the names and functions of each food group. Talk about making good choices, allowing that at times we all eat junk food.

Spotlight on Nonfiction Strategies

- ✹ Activate prior knowledge
- ✹ Generate vocabulary
- ✹ Understand vocabulary in context
- ✹ Build content knowledge base
- ✹ Classify and categorize
- ✹ Question and comment

WHAT THIS SOUNDS LIKE

Every day people make choices about what to eat. Your parents help you decide, too. Yesterday, I ate a big piece of cake at a birthday party. But I don't do that every day, because I want to be healthy. So most of the time I choose salad, cheese, fruit, and other healthy foods.

We have ways of knowing which food is good for us. Some experts made a chart, or guide, to help remind us to eat the right foods each day. This is a food guide because it guides us to make good food choices, and it is called "MyPlate."

Possible Prompts:

- *What do you think you'll see on the guide?*
- *What do you eat that is good for you?*
- *What do you eat that is not so good for you?*
- *Talk to a partner. What's a food that's good for you?*
- *Can you name a food that is a protein? A fruit? A vegetable?*

■ Step 2: Sort Food Picture Cards (1 day)

Point out the six posters for the basic food groups that you have displayed. Pair students and give a set of Food Picture Cards to each one. After modeling an example, have students look at an illustration, read its name, and try to figure out which food group that Food Picture Card belongs to (fruit, vegetables, grains, protein, dairy, or junk food) and then tape it on the corresponding poster. End the activity by looking at the posters and identifying the foods in each group.

WHAT THIS SOUNDS LIKE

Before the sort: *We have learned so much about healthy food. Now let's see if we can find out which group these foods belong in. I've put a food-group poster at each table. We've added a section that's not on the healthy food group chart: junk food. That means food that's not as healthy, such as sweets. The best foods have nutrients to help our bodies stay strong. Junk food doesn't help our bodies; it can even be harmful if you eat too much of it. Let's read the titles: FRUITS, VEGETABLES, GRAINS, PROTEIN, DAIRY, and JUNK FOOD. We're going to use the posters to play a sorting game. You and your partner will get a Food Picture Card, and you will decide which poster it belongs on.*

Let me show you an example. Marla has a peach. Does anyone

> ✶ **REMINDER** ✶
>
> SEND HOME THE
> PARENT LETTER WITH
> CHILDREN TODAY.

Kindergartners sort food pictures.

know which food group a peach belongs to? Talk to your partner and decide. Yes, it's a fruit! So we would put Marla's picture on the fruit poster. Look at and read each Food Picture Card, decide which group it belongs to, and tape the card to that poster.

During the sort: *Remember that the food group guide can help you decide where a card belongs. It also helps to look at a poster and see which foods are already on it. Does your food belong in that group?* (As I listen in, I might say something such as the following: "Let's see, this card shows brown rice. Brown rice is a plant that grows in a field. It's a grain. Can you find that group?" or "Brown rice is a food like bread or wheat, so it's a . . .?")

After the sort: *Look at the fruit poster. Wow! There are so many fruits! Let's name them.* (Repeat this process with each poster.) *Were there any Food Picture Cards that were tricky? Let's talk about where they would go. Tomorrow, we'll look at our own snacks to figure out the food groups we eat. Remember to give the letter in your backpack to your parents tonight.*

Possible Prompts:

- *What kind of food do you think this is?*
- *This is like an apple, it's a ____. (fruit)*
- *This is made of milk so it's ____. (dairy)*

■ Step 3: Sort snacks at six stations (1 day)

Set out food-group posters to create six stations. Place a MyPlate food guide at each station. Repeat yesterday's sort using the snacks that children brought in and the empty wrappers you've collected. Help students sort out snacks, such as granola bars, that may fit into more than one group. Assist them in categorizing tricky ones. Discuss these foods after the sort to clear up misconceptions. Repeat this sort if the class needs more practice.

WHAT THIS SOUNDS LIKE

Before the sort: *Remember the fun sort we did yesterday? Well, now we'll do the same thing sorting wrappers from some of our snacks. I wonder which food groups we eat for snacks? There is an empty food-group poster at each station. You and your partner will tape snack wrappers and plastic bags of sample food to the matching food-group poster. Remember, the MyPlate food group guide is here to help you.*

During the sort: *Do you know what food that is? Let's look at the MyPlate food guide to help. Do you see where that food goes? Can your partner help you? Oh, that's a zucchini squash. That's like a cucumber. It's another kind of vegetable.*

> **Tip:**
>
> ✔ *To make snack collection quick and easy, have each child put his snack at his or her table. Walk around and label them with a marker. Empty snack wrappers can be collected in a central basket for cleaning before they are attached to the charts. If children have a snack without a wrapper, such as carrots, put them in small plastic bags. You can also leave sticky notes on each table and at snack time have children draw a picture of the snack. After snacktime, start the sort using plastic bags or sticky-note drawings, wrappers, and real snacks. You may want to add a few snacks of your own to represent foods to know about, such as fresh fruit, raw veggies, or whole grain crackers.*

After the sort: Let's look at the posters we made today. You guys did great thinking to figure out where these snacks belong! When you bring other snacks this week, we'll add them.

■ Step 4: Review food groups by reading from baskets (2–3 days)

Encourage children to expand their knowledge of food groups through reading books, magazines, and food labels. Keep the posters, food guide, and nutrition word wall on display for easy reference. During transitional times, such as lining up for lunch or dismissal, reread word-wall words. When you gather at the rug for a class meeting, these words can also be reviewed.

WHAT THIS SOUNDS LIKE

There are many places to learn about foods. In the baskets, you'll see books and magazines, and labels from foods. You'll have about 10 minutes to look at this reading material to learn about healthy eating. Read with a partner and talk, remembering to think about which group the food you read about belongs to, and if it's healthy. Remember to use the MyPlate food guide to help you. You can look at the classroom chart (provide individual copies if you wish).

Possible Prompts:

• *What food is this? Name it.*

• *Can you find a fruit, such as an apple? What other fruits are there?*

• *Oh, that's a ____. Do you know which food group it's part of?*

• *Do you like foods in this group?*

 BACK TO EARTH! (4–6 DAYS)

Integrate the experience

Reinforce sorting and nutrition often. We all love food, and now it's easier than ever to remember to eat healthy foods.

■ WRITING CONNECTION: Create Small Books For Rereading (1–2 days)

Before writing: Work with children to decide on a title and a sentence pattern for the book. Write sample sentences on the board. The first sentence might start with a child's name or that of a group; the second sentence tells which group the food belongs to:

> *I ate a ____. That's a ____.*
>
> *Susie likes to eat ____. That's a ____.*
>
> *Some children eat ____. They are ____.*

Spotlight on Nonfiction Strategies

✹ Understand vocabulary in context
✹ Build content knowledge base
✹ Categorize and classify

Then, as a class, create an ending page. This may be a summary page; for example: *We all eat food!* You can also use the last page to rename the food groups (e.g., *We eat fruits, vegetables, grains, protein, and dairy all day long.*) Look at a familiar big book to help you decide.

During writing: Have each child write and illustrate a page about his or her snack for the book. Use paper with a picture box and room for writing sentences. Or try this during interactive writing and do a page a day for each child. (This will take as many days as there are children.)

After writing: Compile children's pages into a book for rereading. You can type the sentences or rewrite them with correct spelling. Make five or six copies for children to reread at independent reading time. They are always pleased to see their own books emerge, and they eagerly share them with parents.

WHAT THIS SOUNDS LIKE

We just learned so much about our snacks. Let's write a book to teach others. Let's write about what we eat for a snack. What could we call our book? We'll use the same pattern for each page so it sounds like the books we read. Daniel, what did you have for snack? What food group was it? (Listen to the response and use the child's sentence structure.) *Daniel just said "I ate a pear. It's a fruit." That can be our pattern. Watch us I write it: I ate a _____. It's a _____. Each of you will write these sentences to tell about your snack. Then draw a picture of it in the picture box.*

■ Learning Extension Activities

CREATE IDEAL MEAL PLACEMATS (1–2 DAYS)

Give a copy of the Ideal Meal Placemat reproducible to each child. Tell students to combine their favorite foods to create an Ideal Meal, one that is healthy with balanced food groups!

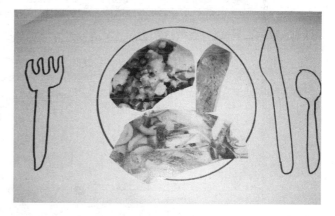

- Set out magazines with food pictures.

- Have children cut out and glue food pictures on the plate for a balanced meal. Then they label the food and food groups on their plate.

- You can laminate the completed reproducibles for use as placemats. (optional)

SET UP A RESTAURANT CENTER (ONGOING)

Young children love pretending—to be a doctor, a teacher, a parent! Play reinforces the learning of names of foods and food groups. In a play restaurant, they can practice acting out the parts of the wait staff, owner, or customer. Gather actual menus, pretend or real snacks, placemats, utensils, and napkins. Create healthy and junk food menus for children to compare. The food is pretend, but the learning is real!

DESIGN FOOD GROUP COLLAGES (2 DAYS)

To reinforce sorting, have children make a food group collage by gluing magazine pictures of a designated food group on a sheet of paper. To reinforce the idea of making healthy choices, ask students to fold the piece of paper in half and glue healthy foods on one side and junk foods on the other.

■ Check in to Evaluate

1. Can students name food groups and classify some foods?

2. Can students find information in reading material related to food and nutrition?

3. Can students make healthy food choices?

■ Home-School Connection

Both teachers and families share the responsibility for good nutrition. Help your students' families integrate the key findings from this nutrition study to home life. The parent letter recommends tips and activities to learn about nutrition and to help children read to make healthy food choices. Consider recommending the following activities as the opportunity arises or through a monthly teacher newsletter:

- Start a family food diary for kids to keep track of their healthy choices.

- Encourage parents to provide healthy snacks for snack time.

Successful Differentiation

Supports:
- Decide on selected snacks to sort.
- Use MyPlate food guide with examples on the plate for reference.

Challenges:
- Plan a healthy menu.
- Write about healthy eating for a blog or Web site.

■ Reproducibles

PARENT LETTER (This is a quick note to send home to parents before the snack sort for the Sort Healthy Snacks adventure. Fill in the actual words from your Healthy/Unhealthy Foods Chart.)

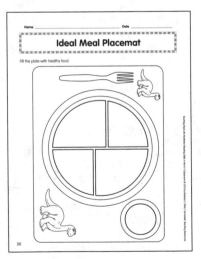

IDEAL MEAL PLACEMAT

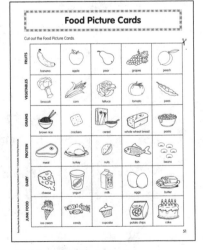

FOOD PICTURE CARDS

Healthy Snacks

Dear Parents,

We are studying healthy foods and the nutritional food guide. We'll notice our snacks in class, so please make sure that your child has a healthy snack to eat each day. We brainstormed and came up with the following healthy list:

_____

_____

As we learn to sort and classify, we will sort our snacks into food groups.

We need your help!

Please send a healthy snack with your child on _____ .

(date)

Please talk about additional snacks your child might like.

What you can do . . .

• Try some new kinds of fruits or vegetables!

• Visit places such as health food stores, grocery stores, and green markets to acquaint your child with new and different foods.

• Continue to name foods you eat and their food groups.

• Later on, use the Ideal Meal Placemat to remind you and your family of good choices. (Your child will be bringing this placemat home soon!)

As always, many thanks for your cooperation.

Your Child's Teacher,

Ideal Meal Placemat

Fill the plate with healthy food.

Food Picture Cards

Cut out the Food Picture Cards.

FRUITS	banana	apple	pear	grapes	peach
VEGETABLES	broccoli	corn	lettuce	tomato	peas
GRAINS	brown rice	crackers	cereal	whole wheat bread	pasta
PROTEIN	meat	turkey	nuts	fish	beans
DAIRY	cheese	yogurt	milk	eggs	butter
JUNK FOOD	ice cream	candy	cupcake	potato chips	cake

Chapter 4

Words Inform Us About Our World: Create a School Newsletter

Children learn how nonfiction is structured while reporting school news.

A Quick Look at Chapter 4

THE ADVENTURE	Collect and study newsletters to learn how to create our own.
READING WORK	Read newsletters. Read a class-generated newsletter.
WRITING CONNECTION	Write parts of the newsletter to be published. Write a poem about the school.
LEARNING EXTENSIONS	Distribute newsletters to the community. Set up a newsletter center. Create a class blog or Web page.
CONTENT-AREA WORK	Key Concepts of a Newsletter Study: • How do people get information? • How do we read newsletters? • Where can we find newsletters? • How do different formats of a newsletter communicate different kinds of information?
PACING	17–22 days

Nonfiction Skills for This Adventure

- **Generate and Apply Background Knowledge**
- **Understand Structure**
- **Learn and Apply Vocabulary**
- **Group Information**
- **Deepen Understanding**
- **Research**

Why Are We Doing This?

Recently, my husband and I discovered a country hamlet. In the quaint café, we read about a farmers' market in the town newsletter. At the market, I joined an e-mail list where I could get updates on local events.

As newsletters and blogs gain in popularity, they ensure that we are always a click away from endless resources. Whatever interests children have—from karate to cupcakes—newsletters are a source of information and entertainment.

In this adventure, students study newsletters to help them create one about their own school. Junior reporters observe, take notes, and write in diverse formats, using mentor newsletters for inspiration. Then, using the fun format of a newsletter, these reporters communicate what they have learned about their school, its people and places. Students recognize wide-ranging formats and embrace the technology of the information age.

 ## COUNTING THE DAYS

What you need

MATERIALS

✓ Books:

- Nonfiction read-aloud selection: *Deadline! From News to Newspaper* by Gail Gibbons
- Fiction read-aloud selection: *The Furry News: How to Make a Newspaper* by Loreen Leedy
- Other related literature: Look for books readers can easily skim for information, making sure texts contain strong visuals, such as the following:

  The Young Journalist's Book: How to Write and Produce Your Own Newspaper by Nancy Bentley

  The Newspaper King by Gardner Wood

  The Paperboy by Dav Pilkey

✓ Reproducibles:

- Parent Letter, p. 64 (1 copy for each family)
- Newsletter Template, p. 65 (1 copy for each child)
- Press Pass, p. 66 (1 copy for each child)

✓ Other Materials:

- clipboards (1 for each child)
- chart paper and marker
- easel

- index cards
- newsletters from a variety of sources
- paper and pencils
- sticky notes
- digital cameras (optional)

PREPARATION

 1 week before:

- *Gather newsletters to serve as mentor texts. Display them on a large chart.*
- *Prepare stopping points in the literature,* The Furry News. *Flag each job when it is first mentioned. Add it to a chart naming jobs at a newspaper.*

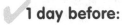 **1 day before:**

- *Set up chart paper on easel.*
- *Collect five or more index cards for classroom labels.*
- *Make copies of the reproducibles.*
- *Place sheets of paper on a clipboard for each child.*

 FUELING UP! (ONGOING)

Activities to keep you going

Newsletters inform readers about services, events, products, and hobbies, connecting with established interests. Use collected newsletters to acquaint students with how they look and what they are about.

- **Browse newsletters.** A week before the adventure, set aside about 10 minutes every day (at snack or center time, for example) for students to browse through newsletters from school and home so they become familiar with them.

- **Teach simple note-taking.** During browsing time, have students use sticky notes to mark places in books where they wonder or learn. Show students how to use tally marks, drawings, or a few words to record questions or facts on the sticky notes. Throughout the study, find two or three times a week to repeat this activity. When students conduct their school interviews in the Lift Off! section, remind them to take notes in a similar way.

Spotlight on Nonfiction Strategies

- ✴ Activate prior knowledge
- ✴ Notice print in varied places
- ✴ Navigate through text features: learn from pictures and photographs
- ✴ Navigate different layouts
- ✴ Use text features as cues
- ✴ Build content knowledge base
- ✴ Preview the text
- ✴ Skim for information

Ready to launch

■ Set a Real-Life Purpose (1 day)

About a week before students undertake their adventure, brainstorm what they know and want to know about school. Organize their responses into a three-column chart as shown below. Generate specific questions about what students want to learn. These will become the basis of their interviews for the class newsletter.

PLACES	PEOPLE	JOBS
How long and wide is the soccer field?	What time does the principal get to school?	Who decides what we eat for lunch?

Spotlight on Nonfiction Strategies

* Connect with a topic
* Activate prior knowledge
* Predict based on prior knowledge
* Navigate through text features: read maps, learn from pictures and photographs
* Build content knowledge base
* Categorize information into groups
* Determine author's purpose
* Skim for information

■ Read Aloud to Learn About Making Newsletters (3 days)

As a prelude to the adventure, I introduce a fiction and nonfiction book about how newspapers are produced.

FICTION READ-ALOUD: *THE FURRY NEWS: HOW TO MAKE A NEWSPAPER* (1 DAY)
Emphasize how people work together to make a newspaper or a newsletter. There are different jobs that involve research, writing, rewriting, and publishing. Explain that in this book, each animal has a function at the newspaper. Focus on how everyone helps and on the jobs you have flagged. Record the jobs on chart paper as students identify them.

NEWSPAPER JOBS	DESCRIPTION	
Editors	Decide what to put in the paper. Read all the parts and make changes.	Give assignments to reporters. Put all the parts together.
Reporters Researchers	Ask questions. Write a headline or title for a story. Check for mistakes.	Find out facts and check them. Research by taking pictures. Research by writing. Research by drawing.
Photographers, Illustrators	Take photos with a camera, or draw pictures.	
Sellers	Sell papers to people.	

WHAT THIS SOUNDS LIKE

Before reading: *We're going to be reporters and find out about our school. We'll share what we learn with our grade and parents. We'll do this by creating a newsletter, just like the ones we collected and have been studying. (Display a newsletter.) We need to do research, write about what we find, then fix our writing and publish the paper. This book will help us learn how to be reporters. It tells about Big Bear, who's in charge of a newspaper. Notice which jobs the animals have. We'll make a list of them.*

During reading: *Put your thumb up when you hear about a job, and I'll write it on our list. Think about the job. Later we'll talk about it. Did you see how the character _____ (took a picture, worked in a team, and so on)? That's what reporters do!*

After reading: *Let's read the list of jobs on the chart. Think about what we would have to do to be reporters and make a newsletter, a small newspaper. Tell your partner which job looks like fun and why.*

NONFICTION READ-ALOUD: *DEADLINE! FROM NEWS TO NEWSPAPER* (2 DAYS)

Explore how newspapers are made in the pages of this book. Acquaint students with the various jobs. Skim the text and visually point out the key parts that correspond to your process of making a newsletter (e.g., the people meeting together, the news being collected, pictures being made, working side by side).

■ Decide on Questions to Research for Newsletter (1 day)

Form committees of reporters (four or five children) to research the questions students have about places, people, and jobs at school. From your chart, choose one question for each committee that is interesting yet can be easily answered through interviews. Create a chart that lists committee members and their questions.

WHAT THIS SOUNDS LIKE

Reporters, I've looked at your questions and picked some for you to investigate for our newsletter. I'll read the questions and names. As you look for answers, you can write notes on paper on a clipboard. Write a word or draw a picture to help you. We are going to have such fun learning more about our school!

> ### Tips
>
> ✔ Include at least one strong writer on each committee.
> ✔ Help committees schedule times for their interviews. Create a calendar showing their interview appointments. If possible, schedule 20-minute interviews across three or four days.
> ✔ Assign an adult volunteer or aide to accompany each committee.

■ Use Mentor Texts to Discuss the Structure of Newsletters (1 day)

Students recognize newsletters from home. Encourage them to notice the different formats used to convey information (e.g., pictures, maps, graphs, surveys, lists, jokes, and so on), which is a useful skill for nonfiction.

WHAT THIS SOUNDS LIKE

We have been looking at newsletters from lots of interesting places. Here's one each from the library, the Little League, and a summer camp. Let's study parts of newsletters and how they look. What can you learn from reading these newsletters?

Possible Prompts:

- *What does this part teach you?*
- *Here's a _____ (list, map, diagram, and so on). What does it represent?*
- *What do people read this newsletter to learn about?*

Children browse sample newsletters.

 LIFT OFF! (8–11 DAYS)

Begin the adventure

Junior reporters don their Press Passes. Off to research!

■ Step 1: Committees research questions (3–4 days)

Before each committee conducts its interview, distribute the Press Passes and have children fill them out. During the interview, have children record what they observe on their clipboards, take photographs if possible, and conduct interviews. (Remember to provide additional adult supervision.)

WHAT THIS SOUNDS LIKE

Now, it's time to find some answers to our questions. Each group has one question to research. Time to fill out your Press Passes! Each day, one group will go with Ms. Reyes, write down what they notice, and the answers to their question. You'll have sheets of paper to draw and write what you see. Later, we'll produce an article or feature for our school newsletter. First we get the information to write about, like Big Bear and the animal reporters!

■ Step 2: Examine sample newsletters to notice different formats (1–2 days)

Display the collection of newsletters. Emphasize that the information in a newsletter can be shared

Spotlight on Nonfiction Strategies

- ✸ Connect with a topic
- ✸ Activate prior knowledge
- ✸ Predict based on prior knowledge
- ✸ Navigate through text features: read maps, learn from pictures and photographs
- ✸ Build content knowledge base
- ✸ Categorize information into groups
- ✸ Determine author's purpose
- ✸ Skim for information

in different ways. Point out where newsletters are from and what kind of format each one uses. Have pairs study and discuss parts of newsletters.

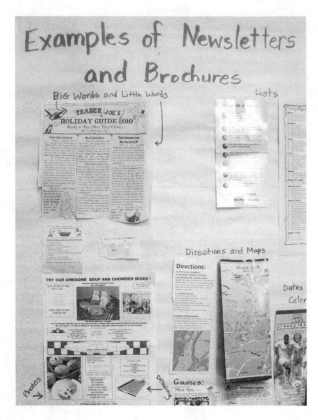

WHAT THIS SOUNDS LIKE

Let's take another look at the newsletters we collected. Information comes in different shapes and sizes! Let's explore how information is presented in different parts of a newsletter. Look, here's an illustration in the Karate Club newsletter. I see the boy holds his hand in a special way. What else can we learn from this picture? Do other newsletters use illustrations? Do you see photographs, too? Both illustrations and photographs give information. Look closely to learn from them.

Let's look at another way to show information. Do you notice anything else in the newsletters? (Take responses.) *Writers decide the best way to show information. To show a place, they might use a drawing or a map. To tell a lot about one person, they would write a story or an article, or make a list. Study these newsletters at your seats and notice how information comes in different forms.* (Allow 10–15 minutes for partners to browse the newsletters and talk about what they notice. Walk around and name the different formats for students. Come together as a class and talk about the different formats students found: maps, picture boxes, diagrams, lists, and so on.)

Possible Prompts:

• *What do you see? (chart, box, picture, graph, list, article, and so on)*

• *What can you learn from this part?*

• *Here is a _____ (calendar, list, map, and so on). What kind of information does it show?*

• *This is a diagram. It shows a shape. What can we learn from the diagram?*

• *What is this part about? How does it teach?*

After the exploration, make a chart of formats that newsletters use. Display real examples next to each format.

Formats:

• *Articles*	• *Maps*	• *Lists*	• *Crossword puzzles*
• *Graphs*	• *Pictures*	• *Photographs*	• *Games*
• *Cartoons*	• *Riddles or jokes*	• *Zoom-in boxes*	• *Fun facts boxes*

■ Step 3: Committees write a part of the newsletter (2 days)

Day 1: Students apply their understanding of formats to write about their research. Ideally, they find a format that matches the information they have to share (e.g., a graph to show how many children are in each grade, or a list to show places to play at school). Have students refer to the list of formats as they decide. You can assign a format if necessary.

When the students in Rebecca Applebaum's class reported how many classes were in each grade, they represented that information as a simple graph. They used sticky notes, and as the photo below shows, the results are easy to read.

Spotlight on Nonfiction Strategies

* Notice print in varied places
* Navigate through text features
* Navigate different layouts
* Categorize information into groups
* Determine author's purpose

WHAT THIS SOUNDS LIKE

You're amazing reporters! You've gathered so much information about our school. Now it's time to put it together. Each committee found information on a different question. Your job is to decide on the best way to share that information. Instead of everyone writing a story or an article, each group can show their information in a different way or format.

For example, a committee counted the number of chairs in the auditorium. Look at the chart of formats and think: What's a good way to show that information? Should they write an article? No, there isn't really much to write about. Should they draw a cartoon? No. That wouldn't be a good way to show the information. Should they make a graph? Hmm. A graph <u>could</u> *show how many chairs are in each row. Graphs show "how many" of something.*

The committee that found out what the librarian does might look at the chart of formats and think: Which format would be best? Their answer might sound like a story or a list of things the librarian does.

Now everyone, talk with the reporters in your committee. Think about your information. Decide which format best matches it. I'll walk around and help. (I write the committee name next to the format on the chart so we will remember.)

Possible Prompts:

- *What do you want to teach?*
- *How can you teach it?*
- *Would a list (map, cartoon, picture, diagram, and so on) help show it best?*

Day 2: For this part, orchestrate each newsletter entry. Take the pictures and words, and cut and paste them to fit the format (e.g. list, article, diagram). I try to do this with the whole class, but realistically some groups may need to meet by themselves, such as the committee doing a graph. The group doing a graph writes each part on a sticky note so it can easily be made into a graph with graph paper. If you need a cartoon, maze, or riddle, ask individual children to do it.

WHAT THIS SOUNDS LIKE

Yesterday you chose your format. This chart shows which format each committee chose. Committee 1 is making a graph; committee 2 is making a list (and so on).

Now I need pictures and sentences from each of you to put together for your section. Then I'll pick some of those for the newsletter.

Look at your interview notes and write one thing you learned. Remember to use your notes. I may ask some children to draw a diagram, or a maze or a cartoon. Raise your hand if you'd like to do that part. The group doing the auditorium graph—you need to write lots of numbers for me so I can put them on the graph. Look at your research and write the numbers you counted. I'll come over and help you. Start by drawing pictures of the chairs you saw.

Possible Prompts:

- *Why don't you draw the ____?*
- *Stella, can you write about the ____, and Ben, can you write about the ____?*
- *Look at the diagram in this book. Can you label your drawing like that?*

■ Step 4: Make a fun facts box (1 day)

As a class, gather facts for a fun facts box for your newsletter. Show samples of this format in familiar books.

WHAT THIS SOUNDS LIKE

Some books contain a special box called Fun Facts. Look at the Fun Facts section in this big book. (Display an example, such as *Apples & Pumpkins* by Melvin and Gilda Berger.) *Let's list facts we know about our school to make a fun facts box to include in our newsletter. Think about true things about our school. I'll start. The music teacher wears sneakers every day.*

And three children in our class have new babies in their families. What else do you know or want to know? We'll write a list called "Did you know?".

Possible Prompts:

• *Think about your interview. What did you notice that can be a fun fact?*

• *What did you notice about the person you interviewed?*

■ Step 5: Compile final newsletter (1–2 days)

You are the final editor of the newsletter, making necessary changes and compiling the information. I shrink children's writing to fit the Newsletter Template (p. 65). I often retype their words so they're readable and the spelling is correct. Then I cut and paste the articles in place. The newsletter is short (one to two pages) and is relatively quick to put together. You can leave space for a class poem (see Writing Connection). Parents may also be available to help.

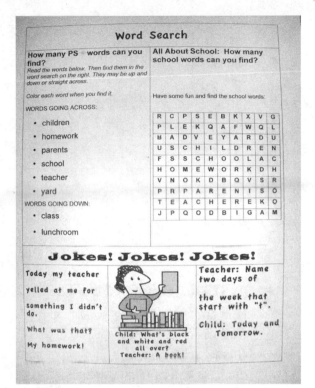

Teacher-generated page

 BACK TO EARTH! (3–5 DAYS)

Integrate the experience

News is all around us. Keep up-to-date with news as it happens!

■ WRITING CONNECTION: Write a Poem About School (2 days)

Have students create a class poem. Use it in the current newsletter or a future one. Set up chart paper at the meeting area to capture students' ideas. Base the poem on their school research.

Spotlight on Nonfiction Strategies

* Build content knowledge base
* Generate new vocabulary
* Understand vocabulary in context
* Classify
* Determine importance

WHAT THIS SOUNDS LIKE

Let's write a poem about what we learned about school from our research. I know you've heard many poems. Now let's try one for our newsletter! We'll write it together. Here's the first line: Our school . . . Can you tell me something our school has? (List ideas, one on each line.)

> **Examples:**
>
> | | |
> |---|---|
> | *Our school.* | *Our school is so much fun* |
> | *523 children* | *The school is made of brick.* |
> | *But best of all . . .* | *The school guard watches out* |
> | *A rooftop jungle gym* | *for everyone.* |
> | *Our school.* | *Our school is so much fun.* |

On the next day, have children draw pictures to illustrate the poem. Be ambitious—let students create personal poems about school.

■ Learning Extension Activities

CIRCULATE NEWSLETTERS (1–3 DAYS)

Find authentic vehicles for rereading. Like a real paper, distribute newsletters for all to read (home, school buddies, staff, community)! Students can run a newspaper stand and hand out copies or stuff mailboxes to distribute to faculty.

UPDATE THE NEWSLETTER (ONGOING)

Real newsletters are published regularly. Establish a consistent publication date for your newsletter. Keep an eye open for newsworthy information. Include work from all facets of school: artwork to celebrate, news about class pets, or a calendar of upcoming events.

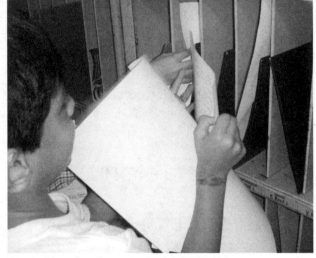

A student distributes a newsletter.

To assure variety, add a new feature for each publication. Try a recipe (e.g., spiced cider for October), a poem about school workers, or a comic strip. Be adventurous! It is valuable for students to see different forms of nonfiction text in an accessible, enjoyable way.

CREATE AN ONLINE EXPERIENCE (ONGOING)

Speak to the school tech guru or a parent for ways to make this an ongoing, predictable structure.

• *Get online!* Can the computer teacher help post the newsletter on the school Web site? Put the word out to relatives and friends. Kids love seeing their writing online!

• *Create a blog!* With technical help, create a blog; for example, older students can ask questions to younger students. Blogs invite comments, praise, and interaction, acting as a motivator for research and more informational writing. Don't overcommit—a blog two even or three times a year can be a highly motivating experience.

Teaching Real-Life Nonfiction Reading Skills in the K–1 Classroom © 2013 by Barbara S. Pinto • Scholastic Teaching Resources

- *Find links of value!* For both Web sites and blogs, information can be shared and connected to a range of sources.

■ Check in to Evaluate

1. Can students find information in different text structures?

2. Do students use pictures to find information?

3. Can students convey information through different formats?

■ Home-School Connection

Children need practice reading many formats, and in this adventure, they look at brochures and newsletters with parents' help. They examine details in pictures as a source of learning. The parent letter reminds families to encourage children to find reading related to their interests and to read different formats. Use the following suggestions to increase parental involvement:

- Send home a sample newsletter for students to add detailed pictures

- Have students write a feature article about their family.

■ Reproducibles

PARENT LETTER (This is a quick note to send home to ask parents to contribute different types of newsletters for this study.)

NEWSLETTER TEMPLATE

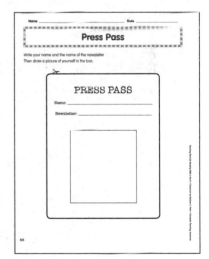

PRESS PASS

Class Newsletter

Dear Parents,

We are learning about how people use newsletters to communicate. Then we will create our own class newsletter. Our class reporters are excited about the terrific newsletter that will come from our research.

We need your help!

Please send in samples of newsletters. You'll find these in all areas of interest, such as newsletters from sports clubs, camps, entertainers, libraries, work, and so on. We need the newsletters soon so we can study them and make our own.

Final collection date is _____ .

What you can do . . .

- Ask your child about the different jobs at a newspaper (reporter, editor, researcher, photographer, seller).

- Look for newsletters when you go on outings (events, museums, scouts, and so on). Read them with your child.

- Monitor the Internet for newsletters on kids' topics.

- Later, read over our class newsletter. (Coming home soon!) Notice all the different formats used.

As always, many thanks for your cooperation.

Your Child's Teacher,

Teaching Real-Life Nonfiction Reading Skills in the K–1 Classroom © 2013 by Barbara J. Fine · Scholastic Teaching Resources

Newsletter Template

Press Pass

Write your name and the name of the newsletter.

Then draw a picture of yourself in the box.

PRESS PASS

Name: _____

Newsletter: _____

Symbols Guide Us in New Places: Use a Map on a School or Neighborhood Treasure Hunt

Children learn map skills as treasure hunters.

A Quick Look at Chapter 5

THE ADVENTURE	Go on a treasure hunt by following clues and using a map; follow up by learning about symbols.
READING WORK	Read directions on a map. Read clues and follow them. Read symbols on a map
WRITING CONNECTION	Use map and photos from the treasure hunt to create a treasure hunt guide.
LEARNING EXTENSIONS	Create a new symbol for the treasure hunt map. Design a school or neighborhood map that shows imaginary places.
CONTENT-AREA WORK	Key Concepts of a Map Study: • What are maps for? • How do map keys help us? • How do you read maps?
PACING	12–13 days

Nonfiction Skills for This Adventure

- **Generate and Apply Background Knowledge**
- **Understand Structure**
- **Learn and Apply Vocabulary**
- **Group Information**

Why Are We Doing This?

I learned to use a map successfully on my honeymoon in Italy, navigating as we drove through the countryside. At first I didn't use the map scale, which indicates distance. I thought what was an all-day trip would be an hour or two! I'm sure I was taught about reading a map in school, but I had never applied the skill. Over the years though, I became a regular navigator, constantly consulting maps. Using maps made me comfortable and proficient with them.

In this adventure, maps lead the way! Children follow clues to relevant places. Reading maps comes naturally to these young treasure hunters as they discover the map key and its symbols during this engaging adventure. Whether you explore your school or the surrounding neighborhood, this instructional treasure hunt will foster map-reading skills.

COUNTING THE DAYS

What you need

MATERIALS

 Books:

- Nonfiction read-aloud selection: *Reading Maps* by David Rhys

- Literary nonfiction read-aloud selection: *On a Treasure Hunt* by Rachel Elliott

- Other related literature: Look for books with a good variety of clear, simple maps, such as these titles:

    As the Crow Flies: A First Book of Maps by Gail Hartman and Harvey Stevenson

    Me on the Map by Joan Sweeney and Annette Cable

    Our Book of Maps by David Flint

Reproducibles:

- Parent Letter, p. 77 (1 copy for each family)

- Map Grid, p. 78 (See Preparation notes on next page.)

- Treasure Hunt Recording Sheet p. 79 (1 copy for each student)

Other Materials:

- a variety of maps from students

- a basket of map-related texts (books, maps)

- a map of school or community (display copy and 1 copy for each student; see Preparation notes on the next page.)

- chart paper and marker

- sticky notes

- strips of paper for treasure hunt clues

- clipboards (1 for each student)
- disposable camera
- treats for the treasure hunt (1 per student, optional)

PREPARATION:

✔ 1 week before:

- *Collect maps and post on a chart* (begin one to three weeks before study).
- *Copy the Parent Letter reproducible and send one home with each student.*
- *Prepare stopping points in the book to be read. Flag places in* On a Treasure Hunt *that show how the girl uses the map and how the clues lead her.*
- *Use the Map Grid reproducible to create the following maps and keys: a display map of an imaginary place for the Fasten Your Seat Belts! section; a map of the school or neighborhood for the treasure hunt in the Lift Off! section.* (Make a display copy and a copy for each student.)
- *Fill in the symbols on the Treasure Hunt Recording Sheet on the treasure hunt map and the key; make a copy for each student.*
- *Write clues for the treasure hunt.* (The first clue should be set in the classroom.) (1 set per group)
- *Organize chaperones for the treasure hunt.*
- *Confirm the locations and schedule for the treasure hunt with the people involved; determine whether it's possible for them to provide treats to children; provide treats yourself otherwise.*
- *Take pictures of places to visit.*

✔ 1 day before:

- *Set out baskets of books and maps.* (1 per table)
- *Drop off clues at each treasure hunt location; confirm schedule.*

Activities to keep you going

Remind students of all they have learned about school on their adventures. There's still so much more to learn!

Read from baskets of map-related material. Give students ample time to peruse maps and the books that feature maps. Doing this even two or three times a week for 5–10 minutes will help them learn the usefulness of maps. Ask partners to talk about what they notice as they look over the material.

You might use the following prompts: *Why do you think people use maps? What kind of map is this? What could this symbol on the map be for? How would you use a map like this?*

Practice map skills. On field trips, secure maps to refer to model so students see how you use them regularly.

Spotlight on Nonfiction Strategies

* Connect with a topic
* Activate prior knowledge
* Apply background knowledge
* Notice print in varied places
* Navigate through text features: read maps

Ready to launch

■ Set a Real-Life Purpose (1 day)

A week prior to the adventure, evaluate students' prior knowledge through a discussion of what they already know about their school (or neighborhood). List their ideas on chart paper. Then discuss how people in a school or neighborhood help each other.

WHAT THIS SOUNDS LIKE

Today, we are going to talk about our school (or neighborhood) and how people help each other here. Let's think about the different jobs that people at school (or in the neighborhood) have. At school, someone makes sure we have heat in the building, someone makes sure we follow the rules, someone cleans the floors, and so on. Soon, we're going to use a map to visit places in our school (or neighborhood) and find people with important jobs. It will be a treasure hunt! Right now, let's list some jobs in our school (or neighborhood). Later, we'll use a map to find where these jobs happen.

Spotlight on Nonfiction Strategies

* Connect with a topic
* Activate prior knowledge
* Apply background knowledge
* Notice print in varied places
* Navigate through text features: read maps
* Generate new vocabulary
* Classify

Possible Prompts:

- *What are some things that people do in our school (or neighborhood)?*
- *When we need something (to be fixed, if a child is sick, a decision needs to be made, some copies made), to whom do we speak? Where do these people work?*

■ Read Aloud to Explore Using Maps (2 days)

FICTION READ-ALOUD: *ON A TREASURE HUNT* (1 DAY)

This book describes a treasure hunt and how clues lead to treasure. Before reading, find out what students know about treasure hunts. Show the grid map used in the book and explain how it works. Remind students that they're going to have their own treasure hunt in the school (or neighborhood), using a map.

WHAT THIS SOUNDS LIKE

Before reading: *The girl in this book is going on a treasure hunt to find her birthday present. She uses a map to help her. On the cover is a picture of the map. She has to follow one clue, which leads to another clue, and at the end, the final clue leads to her present. Doesn't that sound like fun?*

During reading: *See how the map works? The numbers and letters show a place. Let's see how she follows the clues. Oh look, the clue is on the tree (page 5). It tells her to go to a new place. Let's keep reading. On a treasure hunt, each clue leads you to the next place.*

After reading: *The girl in the story did a good job of using the map to find each place. When we have our treasure hunt, we'll use a map and follow clues, too.*

NONFICTION READ-ALOUD: *READING MAPS* (1 DAY)

This book shows locations in two different ways: through photographs and through maps. The maps range from simple maps of rooms to a globe. *Reading Maps* can be used to illustrate how maps are pictures or models.

■ Share and Talk About Maps (2 days)

Spend several days making sure that children understand how maps work. Start by having them view the maps they've brought in and that you've displayed. Talk about what they notice (e.g., squiggly lines, words, a key, it folds, little pictures). Then discuss how maps help us. List students' ideas on a chart like the one shown below.

What We Know About Maps
Maps show real places.
Maps help us if we're lost.
Maps show us all the parts of a place.

WHAT THIS SOUNDS LIKE

As part of our adventure, we're going to use a map to find our way. Here are some maps that you brought in. Wow! Look at all the different kinds. I know many of you have been looking at these maps this week. What did you notice? This is a map of the museum. Here is a map of our school, and here is a map of the park. How are all these maps alike? How could we use them? Tomorrow, we'll talk more about something else that all maps have.

Possible Prompts:

• *What do you see on the map?*

• *Do other maps have that feature, too?*

• *How can this map help you?*

• *When would you use this map?*

■ Explain a Map Key (1 day)

Show the display map of the imaginary place that you created. Focus students' attention on the map key. Explain that each symbol represents a place on the map. Remind children that symbols on maps are simple shapes. This makes the symbols easy to understand and to find on the map. All maps have lines, a key, and symbols.

WHAT THIS SOUNDS LIKE

Here's a simple map with pictures. These pictures are called symbols. They stand for a place in the real world. For example, a square stands for a store. It would be too hard to draw a real store in this little space! This box on the map is called the map key. It tells us what each symbol means. Let's look at parts of the map. What other symbols do you see? How do we know that a circle stands for a house? (Point to the symbol on the map key.) *We'll be using a map with a map key like this when we go on our treasure hunt.*

Possible Prompts:

• *What shape, or symbol, do you see on the map?*

• *Can you find that shape, or symbol, in the map key?*

• *Look, the shapes, or symbols, are the same. Let's read the word next to the shape in the map key.*

• *Can you find the park on the map? Look at the map key first and find the word* park. *Then see which shape is next to it. Next, find that shape on the map.*

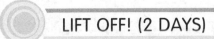

Begin the adventure

During this adventure, focus on the treasure hunt, applying map skills as you go. Keep the activity lighthearted and emphasize teamwork.

Spotlight on Nonfiction Strategies

* Predict based on prior knowledge
* Navigate through text features: read maps
* Acquire nonfiction-specialized vocabulary
* Classify

■ Step 1: Introduce Treasure Hunt map (1 day before the hunt)

Present the display copy of your Treasure Hunt map and distribute a copy of the map to each child. Pair students and connect what they know about maps to study the map they are going to use on their treasure hunt tomorrow. Although the entire class goes on the treasure hunt, having partners makes the guessing more game-like and fun.

WHAT THIS SOUNDS LIKE

This is a map of our school (or neighborhood). We'll use it tomorrow on our special hunt to find the treasured locations. We'll use the chart of jobs (reread the chart) and follow clues to find where people at school (or in the neighborhood) work. Some of our friends have surprises for us, too!

Let's get to know this map. Look at the symbols. Use the map key to figure out what the symbols stand for. Oh look, here's a triangle with a dot inside. Put your finger on it. Now find this symbol in the map key. Read the word next to it with your partner. What is that shape in the real world? Yes, the triangle with the dot inside stands for the principal's office! Let's pretend we're going there and draw a line in the air to get there: We go up the stairs and around the corner. Good. (Repeat this process with each symbol.)

■ Step 2: Set out on the treasure hunt (1 day)

Go over the steps of the treasure hunt:

* Students find a clue and read it.
* They think about which place the clue describes and then use the map key to find that location on the map.
* They use the map to find that location and their next clue.

Distribute the maps, Treasure Hunt Recording Sheets on clipboards, and pencils (and disposable cameras, if available), then work together in the classroom to find the first clue to understand how the treasure hunt works. Then, when the class goes on the hunt, parent helpers assist their assigned team to read and figure out subsequent clues.

WHAT THIS SOUNDS LIKE

We're almost ready to go out and start our treasure hunt! I can't wait, can you? Let's go over the Treasure Hunt Recording Sheet. First of all, there's one clue for each place. The team works together to figure out the location. Each team of four has a parent to help. Using the map to guide us, we'll walk together and stop when we find the place. When we get to a place, you'll have time to write the name of it down. Do your best to copy the sign or write the word. We'll say hello to the people there and then get a new clue. If you are a photographer, please take a picture of each place.

Let's try the first clue together. A clue is like a question, and we need to think of a good answer (Read aloud the clue.) *Think about what place it could be.*

Possible Prompts:

• *Listen to the clue; where do you think this place could be?*

• *Find the shape (symbol) for that place on your map key.*

• *What place did you find?*

• *What can you get or do there?*

• *Who works there? What do they do?*

• *Look at the map. How do you get there?*

> ### Sample Clues
>
> ✔ Where does food get cooked every day? (lunchroom)
> ✔ Where do children play, run, and climb? (playground)
> ✔ Where are there millions of words in one room? (library)

During the treasure hunt, be sure to monitor children to make sure each one has written some words or pictures on the Treasure Hunt Recording Sheet and feels successful. Children may feel pressured to record or become distracted because they are out of the classroom. Provide ample time for students to write, and assure them they can finish later. When you return to the classroom, give 5–10 minutes for children to complete their drawings and words.

Integrate the experience

■ WRITING CONNECTION: Create a Treasure Hunt Guide (2–3 days)

During interactive writing time, write sentences about the places students visited on the treasure hunt, such as the following:

Here's the basement. That's where the boiler gives us heat. Our custodian works here.

Here's the library. That's where we get books to borrow. Our librarian works here.

Add photographs that students took to create pages for your Treasure Hunt Guide. This way, anyone visiting the school can read about your community. Include the map of the school (or neighborhood) and put a star sticker for each place your class visited.

You might fold the guide like a brochure or bind it with spiral binding.

■ Learning Extension Activities

LABEL THE KEY ON THE RECORDING SHEET (1 DAY)

Review each place and corresponding symbol on the treasure hunt map. Work with children to create a new symbol for your classroom and add it to the map key and map.

DESIGN AN IMAGINARY SCHOOL (OR NEIGHBORHOOD) MAP (1 DAY)

Distribute a copy of the Map Grid (p. 78) to each child. Have students work individually or in pairs to design a map that shows three or four places they wish their school or neighborhood had (e.g., a rock climbing room, a swimming pool). Remind students to create symbols for each place and include them in the map key.

■ Check in to Evaluate

1. Can students accumulate information from clues?

2. Can students read map symbols?

3. Can students use maps to find their way?

Spotlight on Nonfiction Strategies

✴ Navigate text features: read a map

✴ Understand vocabulary in context

Riddle for Treasure Hunt Guide

■ Home-School Connection

We want our students to be inquisitive and to learn the function of maps in the world. The parent letter explains how families can reinforce the learning of map skills begun in this adventure by doing the following:

- Go on a treasure hunt in their neighborhood. Add imaginary places to their neighborhood map.

- Collect maps of museums and other places they visit, and explore the maps together.

- Discuss students' favorite locations on the treasure hunt adventure.

■ Reproducibles

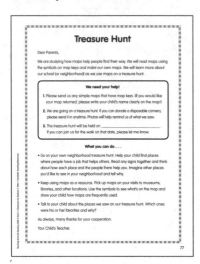

PARENT LETTER (This is a quick note to send home to parents about the school or neighborhood treasure hunt. They are asked to contribute different kinds of maps.)

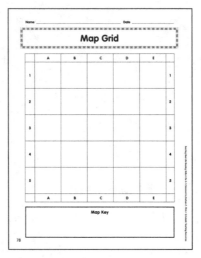

MAP GRID

TREASURE HUNT RECORDING SHEET

Treasure Hunt

Dear Parents,

We are studying how maps help people find their way. We will read maps using the symbols on map keys and make our own maps. We will learn more about our school (or neighborhood) as we use maps on a treasure hunt.

We need your help!

1. Please send us any simple maps that have map keys. (If you would like your map returned, please write your child's name clearly on the map!)

2. We are going on a treasure hunt. If you can donate a disposable camera, please send it in anytime. Photos will help remind us of what we saw.

3. The treasure hunt will be held on _____ . If you can join us for the walk on that date, please let me know.

What you can do . . .

• Go on your own neighborhood treasure hunt. Help your child find places where people have a job that helps others. Read any signs together and think about how each place and the people there help you. Imagine other places you'd like to see in your neighborhood and tell why.

• Keep using maps as a resource. Pick up maps on your visits to museums, libraries, and other locations. Use the symbols to see what's on the map and show your child how maps are frequently used.

• Talk to your child about the places we saw on our treasure hunt. Which ones were his or her favorites and why?

As always, many thanks for your cooperation.

Your Child's Teacher,

Name _____ Date _____

Map Grid

	A	B	C	D	E	
1						1
2						2
3						3
4						4
5						5
	A	B	C	D	E	

Map Key

Teaching Real-Life Nonfiction Reading Skills in the K–1 Classroom © 2013 by Barbara S. Pinto • Scholastic teaching resources

Name _____ Date _____

Treasure Hunt Recording Sheet

Write the name of the place or words you see.

SYMBOL	NAME OF PLACE / WORDS YOU SEE

Chapter 6

Words Help Us Make Choices: Plant a Salad

Children learn how to research, using their green thumbs.

A Quick Look at Chapter 6

THE ADVENTURE	Research and select vegetables to grow for a salad.
READING WORK	Read information on plant-related materials, such as seed packets, catalogs, and books. Research plants; use pictures for information.
WRITING CONNECTION	Design a mural-sized garden diagram with labels. Add captions to the diagram. Add process sentences to the diagram.
LEARNING EXTENSIONS	Write vegetable plant guides and read them. Write a persuasive letter to advocate for planting materials or a school garden. Set up research committees on other topics.
CONTENT-AREA WORK	Key Concepts of a Plant Study: • What kind of plants do we eat? • How do plants grow? What do they need to grow? • How do we take care of indoor plants?
PACING	16–25 days

Nonfiction Skills for This Adventure

- **Generate and Apply Background Knowledge**
- **Understand Structure**
- **Deepen Understanding**
- **Research**

Teaching Real-Life Nonfiction Reading Skills in the K–1 Classroom © 2013 by Barbara S. Pinto • Scholastic Teaching Resources

Why Are We Doing This?

When my sons were young, they made wish lists for holiday and birthday presents. They created them from cut-out catalog and magazine pictures. While these lists helped me shop, my sons benefited, too, because they were reading in a natural, invested way.

Children's enthusiasm for reading is piqued when they have personal input and choice. In this adventure, students are involved in decision making, which gives some power. Reading *can* be hard for some children, so we need to give them real reasons to read.

Get your students' green thumbs ready! They research herbs and vegetables to plant in the classroom by reading seed packets, print magazines, pictures, catalogs, and books. The results are twofold: students learn research skills *and* grow an amazing salad!

 COUNTING THE DAYS

What you need

MATERIALS

✔ Books and Magazines:

- Nonfiction read-aloud selection: *My Bean Plant* by Joseph Ciciano

- Fiction read-aloud selection: *Grow Flower, Grow!* by Lisa Bruce

- Other related literature: Look for books that show the planting process, preferably indoors; books that contain diagrams are preferable, such as the following:

  The Vegetables We Eat by Gail Gibbons

  The Surprise Garden by Zoe Hall

- Articles from magazines such as *Scholastic News* and *Time for Kids*

- Optional big books: Look for photographs that clearly show the growing conditions of plants, such as the following: *Eat Your Vegetables!* by Rosie McCormick (uses fun facts); *Seeds, Seeds, Seeds* by Brian and Jillian Cutting (uses photographs); *Big Red Tomatoes* by Pamela Graham (uses photographs); *This Food Grows Here* by Zoe Sharp (use to add captions); *Animal Eaters of the Pond* by Maud King (uses captions).

Planting Note

Growing plants takes time (1–2 months) and requires sufficient light! Dedicate a sunny spot in your classroom to growing an indoor garden. In this adventure, you're asked to read seed packets with children to gather information, but growing most plants from small flats accelerates growing time. Look for hearty varieties and consult local gardening sources for plants you can grow successfully. Here are some suggestions for your salad garden:
Indoors (choose two or three):
- Head lettuce, baby salad greens, or micro greens
- Tomato plants
- Herbs (basil, chives, parsley)
- Radishes (start from seed: you can eat them when they're small)

Outdoors: cucumbers, carrots, zucchini, squash, corn, and bush bean plants

Supplement your harvest with purchased veggies for salad day—your students will still feel like gardeners! Your goal is to put your research into action.

Tip

✔ *Save children's plant guides from prior studies for future reading.*

Song:

• "What Should We Grow?" (p. 87)

Reproducibles:

• Parent Letter, p. 92 (1 copy for each family)
• Vegetable Picture Cards, pp. 93–94 (1 copy for each pair)

Other Materials:

• chart paper and marker
• mural paper and art materials (paint, crayons, colored pencils, and so on)
• sticky notes
• index cards
• scissors
• camera
• document camera or interactive whiteboard
• basket of plant-related reading material: books, articles, catalogs, seed packets, photographs, and so on
• vegetable and/or herb seed packets (look for packets that have clear pictures and symbols)
• paper towels, plastic bags, and dried lima beans to sprout (1 set for each child)
• vegetable or herb plants, potting soil, pots, tray
• grow lights (if necessary)

PREPARATION

1 week before:

• *Copy Parent Letter reproducible and send home with children.*
• *Copy Vegetable Picture Cards reproducibles and cut apart.*
• *Take photographs of vegetables and label them; include 1 set in each basket.*
• *Prepare stopping points in literature: Flag places in* My Bean Plant *that show how the bean plant is cared for and how it's growing and changing.*
• *Enlarge the directions on a seed packet of vegetables or herbs.* (You may also use a document camera or interactive whiteboard to display the directions.)
• *Copy "What Should We Grow?" song on chart paper.*

1 day before:

• *Set out baskets of plant-related reading material.* (1 per table)

Activities to keep you going

We've studied nutrition, now let's learn to plant healthy foods.

Spotlight on Nonfiction Strategies

✹ Activate prior knowledge

- **Read from baskets of plant books and related materials.** Include songs about planting. Allow time for students to casually browse the seed packets, plant cards, books, and so on, to become familiar with the topic of the adventure.

- **Care for other classroom plants.** Before and after the adventure, give students practice in looking after easy-to-grow plants, such as herbs, coleus, and philodendron.

FASTEN YOUR SEAT BELTS! (3–4 DAYS, + 2 OPTIONAL DAYS)

Ready to launch

"We like to pick the food . . . and eat it too! SURPRISE! We're having a garden party!" (from The Surprise Garden*)*

Spotlight on Nonfiction Strategies

✹ Connect with a topic
✹ Activate prior knowledge
✹ Apply background knowledge to understand a text
✹ Read procedural text: follow a sequence

■ Set a Real-Life Purpose

On the day of the nonfiction read-aloud, explain to children that the vegetables they eat come from seeds and plants that grow. Let them know that they will plant some of their own vegetables in the classroom.

■ Read Aloud to Explore Growing Plants (2 days)

NONFICTION READ-ALOUD: *MY BEAN PLANT* (1 DAY)

About a week before beginning your planting adventure, read this book aloud to demonstrate the stages of a bean plant's growth, day by day. Use the photographs in the text to name the elements needed to grow the plant (earth, seeds, pot, water). Notice what students indicate they already know about plants. Tell children that bean sprouts, like the ones shown, are tasty!

WHAT THIS SOUNDS LIKE

Before reading: *Beans and bean sprouts are good to eat. In this book, we'll see how a bean plant grows. Look at the wonderful photographs; notice how the plant changes every day. We can start our own bean plants to grow for salad! This book shows us the steps to follow to do this.*

During reading: What do you see in this photograph? Look at the seeds, plants, pot, water, and earth. How did the bean plant change?

After reading: It was exciting to see the bean grow into a plant. What else would you like to grow?

FICTION READ-ALOUD: *GROW FLOWER, GROW!* (1 DAY)

Engage students in a discussion about what plants need to live. As you read this delightful story, point out how plants need special care—different from what people need. Have students think about the silly things Fran did. What could she do to give her plant better care? Then discuss the vegetables that students like in their salad. Discuss how these vegetables grow.

■ Discuss Growing Plants and Vegetables (1–2 days)

Day 1: Discuss children's knowledge of plants. If possible, visit a local garden. Distribute a set of the Vegetable Picture Cards to pairs of students. Also encourage them to refer to *My Bean Plant.* Ask children to talk with a partner about what they know about plants. Then ask students to share with the class and chart their responses; a sample chart appears at the right.

WHAT WE KNOW ABOUT PLANTS
They need water.
They need sun.
They need food.
Some grow inside.
Some grow outside.

WHAT THIS SOUNDS LIKE

Remember when we saw our school rooftop garden? There were lots of plants growing. Have you ever grown a plant? Talk to your partner. Tell him or her something you already know about growing plants. Think about how the information in My Bean Plant *can help you. Later, we'll grow some plants here!*

Possible Prompts:

• *Look at this plant. Tell me what you know about how it grows.*

• *Remember our school garden? Think about how vegetables grow there.*

Day 2: To discuss what children know about vegetables and growing them, refer to the MyPlate food guide in Chapter 3. Listen for the background knowledge that children display and which vegetable names they know.

WHAT THIS SOUNDS LIKE

Soon, we're going to grow a salad! What do you think goes into a salad? Let's look at the vegetable list from the food guide sort (Chapter 3). *Some of my favorite vegetables are carrots and lettuce.* (Display the Vegetable Picture Cards.) *What other vegetables do you like in a salad?* (List responses on a chart.)

Possible Prompts:

• (Show Vegetable Picture Cards.) *Have you ever eaten any of these vegetables?*

■ Grow Bean Sprouts (optional) (2 days)

To grow bean sprouts, which need little care, follow the steps pictured in *My Bean Plant*: Have each child soak a dried lima bean in water, wrap it in a wet paper towel, and then place it in a small plastic bag. As the plants develop, work with students to name their parts.

WHAT THIS SOUNDS LIKE

Let's look at My Bean Plant. *Remember how the boy grew his beans?* (Flip the pages to show the steps.) *We're going to follow these steps to grow our own bean plants. Look, we have lima beans, paper towels, and small plastic bags. We'll sprout the beans and eat them in a salad.*

Possible Prompts:

- *Watch as I _____.*
- *This is a _____. What is it used for?*

LIFT OFF! (8–11 DAYS)

Begin the adventure

Students read and research to prepare their green thumbs for planting. Details reveal information to help them make decisions.

■ Step 1: Explore pictures and symbols on a seed packet (1 day)

Display the directions on the packet of vegetable or herb seeds to teach children how to find information. Point out the pictures and symbols and discuss what this information means.

WHAT THIS SOUNDS LIKE

Look at this packet of lettuce seeds. Think: What can I learn about how or when to plant these seeds? We'll be planting small plants, but seed packets can help us learn about how to take care of our plants. See these pictures, or symbols? Remember what we learned about symbols from using the map and map key on our school (or neighborhood) treasure hunt? Seed packets are one of the places to find information about plants. This picture shows the sun. What do you think this other symbol means?

Possible Prompts:

- *What picture do you see here?*
- *What does this picture tell us?*

Spotlight on Nonfiction Strategies

* Activate prior knowledge
* Navigate through text features: learn from pictures and photographs.
* Figure out main idea(s) of a section
* Determine importance
* Find answers to questions
* Preview the text
* Skim for information

■ Step 2: Teach how illustrations and photographs show information (1–2 days)

During browsing/reading time, explore the baskets of plant-related reading material. Ask children to look for illustrations and photographs and talk about the information each one shows. Explain that in nonfiction texts, pictures and photos are essential sources of information.

WHAT THIS SOUNDS LIKE

When we looked at seed packets, we read the symbols to get information. You can use pictures and photographs to find information, too! Let me show you what I mean. Let's look at this picture of a lettuce plant. (Choose a big book with plant photographs, such as *Seeds, Seeds, Seeds* by Brian and Jillian Cutting, or enlarge one of the plant cards.) *I see the plant on a windowsill. It's in a pot with soil. That tells me that lettuce must have sunlight to grow, and that it must grow in soil. In this picture, a girl is watering the plant; that tells me plants need water to grow. I haven't even read the words yet! We read the words to learn more, but first we study the pictures. Look closely. Name what you see, then think about what you can learn. Today, you'll be reading more about plants from the materials in these baskets.*

Possible Prompts:

• *Look closely at the picture. What do you see?*

• *What do you think the picture teaches us?*

• *Where is the plant growing? What else do you notice about it?*

• *What else does the plant need to grow?*

• *Do you see information about the food, light, or water the plant needs?*

■ Step 3: Use note-taking to choose plants to grow (2–3 days)

Continue to have students read plant-related material from the baskets for 10–15 minutes for several days. Encourage them to place a sticky note on pages to show where they learned information or which vegetables they like. Ask them to draw a smiley face on a note to show a plant they want to grow. Children can write information they learned from the picture or words as well. Make a quick list of the vegetables that children choose.

WHAT THIS SOUNDS LIKE

Today, we are going to read more about vegetables. Look at all the different kinds of reading materials in the baskets. You can study the pictures on the seed packet like we did the other day, and the photographs. Or you can look at the Vegetable Picture Cards and read the name of the vegetables and how they grow. (Read one of the plant cards.)

As you read, I want you to think about growing this vegetable in our classroom. If you like a vegetable, put a sticky note on it so we can remember it. Add a smiley face! Tell why you like it. We'll list vegetables we'd like to plant. Some vegetables, such as corn, require a lot of space. But many vegetables can grow in small spaces. We'll pick some of those. We'll choose three to grow right here in our classroom for a yummy salad!

Possible Prompts:

- *Look at the picture. What could it be?*
- *Ask your partner for help to read the words.*
- *Think: Do I like this vegetable in salad?*
- *Think: Could this vegetable grow in our classroom?*
- *Does the picture show how to take care of the plant?*

■ Step 4: Skim a text for planting information (1 day)

With students, look over the list of possible vegetables to plant that you created. Show them how to skim the information from the corresponding Vegetable Picture Cards and seed packets to find out how much space each plant requires. Rule out any vegetables that need too much space. Point out how to skim the text without reading every word. Like weeding a garden, we select what is useful to keep, and put aside the rest!

WHAT THIS SOUNDS LIKE

You've chosen a lot of vegetables that you'd like to grow. Let's see if we have enough space in our room to plant them. How far apart will we have to plant them? Let's use the pictures on the seed packets and Vegetable Picture Cards to help us decide. Then let's skim the words. That means we'll look at the words quickly to see if they tell us that information, too. Can this plant grow in a small garden? Can it grow in a pot instead of in the ground?

Now, I'll read about each vegetable. Put your thumb up if you think this plant doesn't need too much room. Put your thumb down if it does need a lot of space.

■ Step 5: Decide which vegetables to plant (1 day)

Introduce the song "What Should We Grow?" to help children understand how research leads to a decision. If possible, build enthusiasm by taking the class to a local nursery. Listen to children's suggestions for seeds or plants for their classroom garden, and remind them that plants they choose need to have the right growing conditions.

WHAT SHOULD WE GROW? (sing to the tune of "Three Blind Mice")

What should we grow?
What should we grow?
What do we like?
What do we like?

Tomatoes or cucumbers—good for you!
Carrots and lettuce and green beans, too.
Radish, spinach, or mushrooms (ooh)!
That's what we'll grow.

What grows the best?
What grows the best?

What tastes so fresh?
What tastes so fresh?

We need some plants that will live in here.
We need some plants that need our care.
We need to find whatever grows here.
What would be best?

■ Step 6: Plant your salad garden (1 day)

Fill the pots with potting soil and set them out on the tables with the plants. Cover tables ahead of time. Also set out the index cards. Then ask students to work in pairs to pot each plant. Have each group plant a different vegetable. Label it with a word and/or picture with the help of a Vegetable Picture Card. You may devote several tables to one kind of vegetable. Create a Plant Care Chart and ask children to sign up as shown below. Four children will be plant helpers each day.

PLANT CARE CHART					
	Monday	Tuesday	Wednesday	Thursday	Friday
water					
light					
good soil					
plant food					

WHAT THIS SOUNDS LIKE

It's time to start our garden. Each partnership has a small plant to put in a pot. Carefully take the plant out of the container, like this, and place it in the pot. Then take your fingers and pat the soil around. Watch me again. (Circulate as students pot their plants, giving guidance as necessary.)

Now, use the blank card on your table to make a sign. Write your name and the plant name. You can also draw a picture. Remember, the name is on the Vegetable Picture Card. Put the pot on this tray with the plant card. (Collect the pots and attach student labels afterward.) *We'll take turns caring for our plants. Here's a chart to help us. It takes time for things to grow, so we'll have to be very patient!*

■ Step 7: Harvest and eat your salad garden (several weeks to grow, 1–2 days to harvest and eat)

What better way to celebrate your adventure than to eat from your garden! Children who have never eaten salad will clamor to devour their homemade triumphs. While waiting for the crop, try special snacks that include lettuce, sprouts, basil, and chives. Help children appreciate that food takes time to grow.

In the meantime, the Writing Connection and Learning Extension activities below will keep your students busy. Then, when it's time, harvest, wash, chop, and enjoy your salad!

BACK TO EARTH! (5–10 DAYS)

Integrate the experience

Students actively show their understanding as you reinforce the importance of diagrams and illustrations.

■ WRITING CONNECTION: Make a Diagram of the Salad Garden (3–5 days)

PART 1: CREATE THE DIAGRAM (1–2 DAYS)

Have students reconstruct their learning by making a mural-sized diagram of their garden. Follow these steps to teach them how to make a diagram and label its parts:

- Show diagrams from nonfiction big books (e.g., *Eat Your Vegetables* by Rosie McCormick) or enlarge copies from regular-size books (e.g., *Dolphins* by Sylvia M. James).

- Point out features of the diagrams (labels, lines that connect art and text, and specific details).

- Have students work together to create the diagram on a large sheet of mural paper. Help them label the parts of the diagram.

- Find details in the diagram that teach, and point them out (e.g., roots grow underground).

Spotlight on Nonfiction Strategies

- ✳ Notice print in varied places
- ✳ Navigate through text features: read diagrams, learn from pictures and photographs
- ✳ Read procedural text (follow a sequence)
- ✳ Determine importance
- ✳ Find answers to questions
- ✳ Organize information

Diagrams of classroom plants

PART 2: ADD CAPTIONS TO THE DIAGRAM (1 DAY)

Use a big book as a model to teach about captions, such as *Animal Eaters of the Pond* by Maud King. Explain that captions describe, give information, or offer a tip. Writing their own captions for a book such as *This Food Grows Here* by Zoe Sharp shows children the importance of captions: *Look at the trees full of fruit.*

Possible Prompts:

• *What can our diagram teach people?*

• *Think about what we learned about plant care.*

• *What plant tip can we give in a caption?*

PART 3: WRITE PROCESS SENTENCES ABOUT THE DIAGRAM (1–2 DAYS)

Ask students to decide on a few sentences that describe how they created their diagram, such as these:

• *We drew the plants.*

• *We labeled each part.*

• *We made a garden on paper!*

■ Learning Extension Activities

WRITE VEGETABLE PLANT GUIDES AND READ THEM (1–4 DAYS)

Have students use print resources to make simple individual or group plant guides. Tell children to include basics on one page, such as the plant's name, a picture (or photograph), and growing information. Help students design a cover page with a title and an illustration. Add a table of contents and compile the pages into one guide. Make copies to read in class and then send them home, saving one for future plant studies.

WRITE A PERSUASIVE LETTER TO THE PRINCIPAL TO ADVOCATE FOR PLANTING MATERIALS OR A SCHOOL GARDEN (1 DAY)

Capture the spirit of this adventure and show students how knowledge leads to action. Ask students to contribute ideas for a letter to the principal that explains how they chose and grew vegetables. Give one or more compelling reasons why such an activity is beneficial to them and the school.

SET UP RESEARCH COMMITTEES ON OTHER TOPICS (ONGOING)

Encourage children to continue researching other topics. Have them browse books and choose an interest (e.g., dolphins, rocks). Ask them to make a culminating brochure or fact book about their topic. This activity reinforces the following research skills that students have learned:

  • Browsing
  • Note-taking
  • Gathering information from photographs and illustrations
  • Reading diagrams, captions, and headings
  • Talking to a partner to confirm information and understanding

Teaching Real-Life Nonfiction Reading Skills in the K–1 Classroom © 2013 by Barbara S. Pinto • Scholastic Teaching Resources

■ Check in to Evaluate

1. Can students name some plants and describe their care?

2. Can students find information in related reading materials through text features (e.g., diagrams, captions, photographs)?

3. Can students make decisions based on their research?

■ Home-School Connection

We want parents to understand that learning comes from many sources; we read to inform ourselves of choices and to help us make decisions. The parent letter gives options for learning about planting and decision-making. Here are more suggestions for involving parents:

- Invite families to get creative by making salads with different ingredients.

- Ask families to contribute a favorite salad or vegetable recipe to include in a class recipe book.

■ Reproducibles

PARENT LETTER (This is a quick note to bring parents on board by asking them to collect pictures and photographs of plants and to expose their children to plant and vegetable names.)

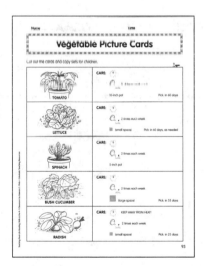

VEGETABLE PICTURE CARDS

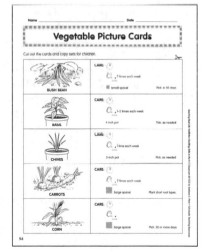

Plant a Salad

Dear Parents,

We are studying plants to find vegetables to grow for a class salad garden. We'll use books, magazines, seed packets, and brochures to research plants and how to care for them. This will help us make informed choices for our garden.

We need your help!

Please send in books, magazines, catalogs, seed packets, or brochures about different kinds of vegetables or planting vegetable gardens.

If you can take photos of salad vegetables, please send them in. If you have information about the plant's growing requirements, write it on the back of the photo. We especially need to know about light, space, and whether the plant can grow indoors.

Please send this material in as soon as possible.

The study starts on _____ .

What you can do . . .

• Reinforce plant names through visits to gardens, parks, and nurseries.

• Use your own research for decision making: what to have for dinner, restaurant reviews, deciding on shopping based on grocery flyers.

• Later on, ask your child how we grew the salad. You might want to try growing your own salad garden at home!

As always, many thanks for your cooperation.

Your Child's Teacher,

Vegetable Picture Cards

Cut out the cards and copy sets for children.

 **TOMATO**	**CARE:**  3–4 times each week 10-inch pot Pick: in 60 days
 **LETTUCE**	**CARE:** 2 times each week (small space) Pick: in 60 days, as needed
 **SPINACH**	**CARE:** 2 times each week 5-inch pot
 **BUSH CUCUMBER**	**CARE:** 2 times each week (large space) Pick: in 55 days
 **RADISH**	**CARE:** KEEP AWAY FROM HEAT! 2 times each week (small space) Pick: in 25 days

Vegetable Picture Cards

Cut out the cards and copy sets for children.

BUSH BEAN

CARE:

 2 times each week

☐ (small space)   Pick: in 50 days

BASIL

CARE:

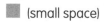 1–2 times each week

4-inch pot   Pick: as needed

CHIVES

CARE:

 1 time each week

3-inch pot   Pick: as needed

CARROTS

CARE:

 2 times each week

▨ (large space)   Plant short root types.

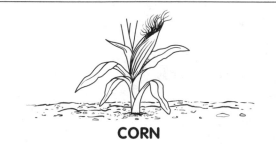
CORN

CARE:

▨ (large space)   Pick: 58 or more days

Chapter 7

Words Teach Us, Step by Step: Make Lemonade

Children learn how to read procedural text and make a beverage.

A Quick Look at Chapter 7	
THE ADVENTURE	Follow directions in a lemonade recipe and in procedural texts.
READING WORK	Read sequential directions. Learn step-by-step reading. Read how-to books.
WRITING CONNECTION	Write a class "1, 2, 3" book to teach in steps. Write individual how to books.
LEARNING EXTENSION ACTIVITIES	Review transitional words. Create class recipes. Re-sequence stories with pictures.
CONTENT-AREA WORK	Key Concepts of Procedural Text (How-to) Study: • What kinds of things can we teach others? • What sequence do we follow? • Which words indicate sequence?
PACING	• 11–12 days

Nonfiction Skills for This Adventure

- **Generate and Apply Background Knowledge**
- **Understand Structure**
- **Learn and Apply Vocabulary**
- **Group Information**
- **Deepen Understanding**
- **Research**

Why Are We Doing This?

When I was little, my friend and I made animals from dyed Easter eggs, following the directions from a magazine: color the eggs, use toothpicks for legs, and draw faces with markers. I had just finished making a pig when we heard a fire engine siren. We ran outside, but I darted back inside to get my precious art project. Though we were safe, my mother warned, "You could always make another pig; we can't make another you!" The fire taught me this valuable lesson: I didn't need to save the pig. I had the knowledge to make a barnyard of animals—but I hadn't yet realized it.

The memory of this experience helped crystallize the understanding that teaching kids the skill to read directions supports them throughout life. We read procedural text often, from product information to recipes.

What youngster doesn't like lemonade? In this adventure, students read and use directions as they cook. They begin to appreciate the relevance of directions for homework, sports, and video games. Sequence matters in oral language, too; for example, "After you wash your hands, we'll have dinner." Directions are everywhere!

COUNTING THE DAYS

What you need

MATERIALS

✔ Books:

- Nonfiction read-aloud selection: *How to Make a Paper Frog* by Jan Pritchett
- Fiction read-aloud selection: *Walk On! A Guide for Babies of All Ages* by Marla Frazee
- Other related literature: Look for books in which an item can be made easily in a how-to center; look for simple steps and clear photographs, such as in the following:

  How to Make Salsa by Jaime Lucero

  Making a Picture by Sara Oldfield

  Make a Paper Airplane by Cathy French

✔ Reproducibles:

- Parent Letter, p. 108 (1 copy for each family)
- Lemonade Recipe, p. 109 (a large display copy and 1 copy for each student)
- How-to Paper, p. 110 (1 copy for each student)

✔ Other Material:

- chart paper and marker
- sticky notes
- baskets of how-to books

- optional "How-to Song"
- ingredients for lemonade: lemons, water, sugar
- utensils: pitcher; strainer; measuring cups; lemon squeezer; large spoon; electric teakettle, hot pot, or microwave to heat water; a paper cup for each child
- small plastic bags
- optional: pitchers, cups, signs, and markers for lemonade stand; access to refrigerator

PREPARATION

✔ 1 week before:

- *Create a large display copy of the Lemonade Recipe reproducible.*
- *Prepare stopping points in literature:* Flag places in *How to Make a Paper Frog* that show numbered steps and note how each step depends on the one before it.
- *Set out baskets of how-to books.*
- *Copy the Parent Letter reproducible and send one home with each student.*

✔ 1 day before:

- *Gather ingredients and utensils for making lemonade.*
- *Cut apart the steps of a Lemonade Recipe reproducible.*
- *Optional: Create a display chart for the lyrics of the "How-to Song":*

  HOW-TO SONG (sing to tune of "Twinkle, Twinkle Little Star")
  When you cook, you follow steps.
  Follow what the recipe says.
  If it's FIRST, then do it first.
  If it's NEXT, then do it next.
  Stay in order, that's my tip.
  FI-NAL-LY you'll have a sip—YUM!

  When you learn, you follow steps.
  Follow what directions say.
  If it's FIRST, then do it first.
  If it's NEXT, then do it next.
  Stay in order, learn it well.
  FI-NAL-LY you'll learn to spell (or read or count). YES!

Activities to keep you going

Decide on a celebration for making lemonade. As an optional extension, you can set up a lemonade stand or decorate the cups you're using—keep this adventure light and fun.

Read from baskets of how-to books. A week before the adventure, allot time for children to become familiar with the how-to books that will later go into a how-to center.

Demonstrate making objects that require following steps (1–2 days, then an ongoing center). Use one of the how-to books in the baskets to show how to complete a task, such as making a snack or planting a seed.

Set up a how-to center. Include the baskets of how-to books and related materials in the center. Have partners use the materials (e.g., paper, clips, markers) to make objects and then draw the steps they followed and add captions.

> **NOTE:** How-to centers can be set up before, during, or after making lemonade. One first-grade teacher created a how-to center weeks before the adventure. She explained, "I wanted my students to follow instructions before nonfiction writing so they'd have a bit of experience using a sequence of steps. And they'll know the books!" A class favorite for the how-to center is making a paper airplane. As they use procedural text, *Make a Paper Airplane* by Cathy French, children become adept at reading how-to books.

Spotlight on Nonfiction Strategies

✴ Activate prior knowledge

Ready to launch

■ Set a Real-Life Purpose (1 day)

Decide on an authentic purpose for making lemonade—as a special snack, a writing celebration, or to welcome spring! A week or two before the adventure, post its date on your class calendar.

WHAT THIS SOUNDS LIKE

We're going to make a special snack to welcome spring! Have you ever tasted lemonade? Did you ever make it yourself?
In a week, on next Friday, we'll follow a recipe to make lemonade and learn how to read directions. What do you think we'll need?

Spotlight on Nonfiction Strategies

✴ Connect with a topic
✴ Generate new vocabulary

◼ Connect with a topic by using other how-tos (same day)

To prepare for making lemonade, teach students about following how-to procedures. Many parts of our lives function well because we learn the sequence of steps to accomplish tasks. Use a classroom example, such as lining up, to give students practice in following the steps to complete a task.

WHAT THIS SOUNDS LIKE

When we make lemonade, we'll follow the steps of a recipe. We often do things in a certain order. For example, we always line up for lunch. Let's practice following the steps for lining up: First, listen for your name. Then, get up and push in your chair. Next, get your lunch. Finally, stand in your spot in the line. Very good! When we cook, we follow the steps of a recipe in order. The recipe tells us what to do first and what to do next. Each number in our lemonade recipe is a step in a procedure or sequence.

Possible Prompts:

- *Can you think of something else we do in a specific order?*
- *We follow steps to cook. When else do we follow steps?*

◼ Read Aloud to Explore How to Follow Steps in a Sequence (2 days)

NONFICTION READ-ALOUD: *HOW TO MAKE A PAPER FROG* (1 DAY)

Tie in the literature by emphasizing how we follow steps, which leads to a finished product. As you read aloud, stop to discuss the places you flagged in the text. Emphasize transitional words, such as *first, next, then, last,* and *finally.*

WHAT THIS SOUNDS LIKE

Before reading: *I am going to read a book that gives you steps to follow. The boy in the book is making a paper frog. He follows each step in the text, in order, and look what he makes! Notice how the book names each step and tells you about it. The pictures show the steps, too.* (Flip pages.)

During reading: *Do you see how the boy does each step, one by one? Find the step numbers. Why is it important to follow steps in order?*

After reading: *Let's remember what happened in this book. What did the boy do first? Next? Last? Use your fingers to show your partner the steps the boy used to make his paper frog.*

FICTION READ-ALOUD: *WALK ON! A GUIDE FOR BABIES OF ALL AGES* (1 DAY)

Focusing on the easily identifiable topic of babies, this story is full of tips on how a baby stands and walks. It delivers the point by breaking a complex act into small steps in a comical way.

■ Illustrate Individual Recipes (1 day)

Have each child illustrate the lemonade recipe. (If you prefer, small groups can illustrate a different part of the recipe.) Show the display copy of the Lemonade Recipe reproducible and then give a copy of it to each child. Read the recipe aloud and tell partners to read it with you, touching each number. Emphasize transitional words (*first*, *then*, *next*, *last*), and review the ingredients before children begin. Then ask partners to retell the recipe to each other.

WHAT THIS SOUNDS LIKE

Here's our recipe for lemonade. Let's look at each number in the recipe and read the steps as I point. First a recipe tells us what we need. Those are the ingredients. Follow along as I read the ingredients. Now put your finger on the number 1. This step says . . . (Read the step.) *This is the first step in making lemonade.* (Repeat for each step.) *Now it's your turn to tell the recipe to your partner. Hold up a finger for each step.*

Possible Prompts:

• *Picture what's happening here.*

• *This is the part when you . . .*

• *What kind of picture would go with this step?*

• *What do we do next?*

LIFT OFF! (3 DAYS)

Begin the adventure

Enjoy making delicious lemonade. Emphasize sequence as you go.

■ Step 1: Talk about the importance of doing things in a specific order and introduce procedural words (1 day)

Introduce a real-life analogy to bring the point home that sequence is necessary. Use transitional words, including *first, then, next,* and *last,* to remind children that order counts!

WHAT THIS SOUNDS LIKE

There are certain things that we can do in any sequence, such as loading a backpack. But some procedures <u>must</u> be done in order, such as getting dressed—underwear before pants and shirt! Our school schedule is listed in order: what we do first, next, then, last. The schedule is like a recipe; we follow it in a specific way. Could I drink lemonade before I squeeze the lemons?

Spotlight on Nonfiction Strategies

✴ Read procedural text: follow a sequence
✴ Acquire nonfiction-specialized vocabulary
✴ Understand vocabulary in context
✴ Generalize information
✴ Visualize what's happening
✴ Skim for information

- *Can you think of something where the order matters?*
- *What do we do _____ (first, last) every day at school?*

■ Step 2: Read the recipe with the class (1 day)

Many children will have had experience making lemonade, but some may not have had the opportunity. Reread the display copy of the lemonade recipe together as shared reading, reviewing the procedure and content. Repeat again throughout the day.

WHAT THIS SOUNDS LIKE

Boys and girls, let's look at our lemonade recipe again. This recipe tells one way to make lemonade. Let's read each part. Which part goes first? There is an order we must follow, and these numbers remind us of that. We always begin with Step 1. Then we do Steps 2, 3, 4, and so on. As I read the recipe, hold up your fingers to show me which step we are on. (Read the recipe while pointing to each step on the display copy.) Do you see how each step fits after the one before it? Good, let's read the recipe again. This time try to read along with me.

Possible Prompts:

- *Which step or number are we on now?*
- *Which step comes next?*

Connect Procedural Work to Retelling in Fiction

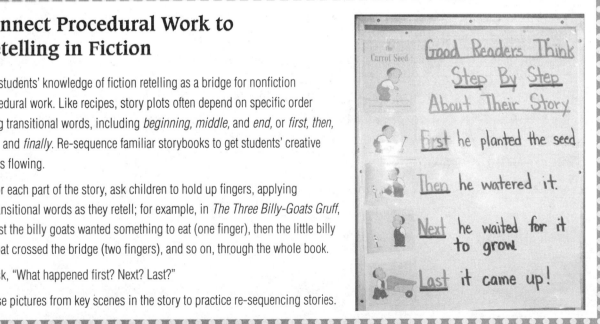

Use students' knowledge of fiction retelling as a bridge for nonfiction procedural work. Like recipes, story plots often depend on specific order using transitional words, including *beginning, middle,* and *end,* or *first, then, next,* and *finally.* Re-sequence familiar storybooks to get students' creative juices flowing.

- For each part of the story, ask children to hold up fingers, applying transitional words as they retell; for example, in *The Three Billy-Goats Gruff,* first the billy goats wanted something to eat (one finger), then the little billy goat crossed the bridge (two fingers), and so on, through the whole book.

- Ask, "What happened first? Next? Last?"

- Use pictures from key scenes in the story to practice re-sequencing stories.

■ Step 3: Dramatize each part of the lemonade recipe (same day)

Before beginning this step, cut apart the steps of the Lemonade Recipe reproducible and shuffle them. Have children use gestures as they repeat the boldface sequence word on the display copy of the lemonade recipe (*first*, *then*, *next*, *after*, *last*) with you to exaggerate the important parts. Then have students reorder their own Lemonade Recipe reproducible.

WHAT THIS SOUNDS/LOOKS LIKE:

Let's move our bodies as we read each step. (Read recipe with gestures.) *Now I'm going to mix up the steps in your recipe. Let's put the recipe parts in order. Let's have five children, one for each step, come up and hold a different part of the recipe. Now stand in the correct order to make lemonade.*

■ Step 4: Review the recipe by skimming (1 day)

Ask young cooks to glance at or skim the recipe in preparation for making lemonade. Show how you skim by looking for important words without reading *every* word. Name times that skimming is helpful; for example, when you gather materials, want to remember what you just read, or look for information. Guide children to skim their individual copies of the recipe as you model skimming the display copy.

WHAT THIS SOUNDS LIKE

Are we ready to begin? I want to use the recipe to help me check for ingredients. I won't read every word; instead, I run my finger down the recipe quickly, looking for what I need. I don't read the entire recipe, I just check to see if I have what I need! It's like skipping some rocks when we walk along a creek; we just step on some important ones. I am skimming, reading quickly, to find what I need. (Skim and name the ingredients.) *Now you try it with your recipes. Then look at each step and find important words such as* lemons, sugar, *and* water. *Skimming helps us get ready to make the lemonade.*

Possible Prompts:

• *Move your finger quickly down the recipe.*
• *Look for these words:* lemons, sugar, water.
• *Can we look over the recipe quickly?*

■ Step 5: Make the lemonade (same day)

It is easiest to make the lemonade as a demonstration, but you can also assign tasks to different groups of children. Refer to the recipe, engaging students' senses and integrating vocabulary. Reread each step clearly (with gestures) from the display copy of the recipe. I set up the classroom as shown below:

- Establish a designated station to squeeze most of the lemons beforehand.
- Demonstrate making sugar water.
- Combine the sugar water with the lemon juice.

Keep track of new words on a specialized word wall, and add words as they are used in context.

WHAT THIS SOUNDS LIKE

Making lemonade is really simple; our recipe tells what to do. We already have what we need: lemons, water, and sugar. That's it! Let's read the recipe to see what comes first. (Read the first step with the class.) *Now we squeeze the lemons. Show me with your bodies how to squeeze tightly. Watch the hot pot as we boil the water. Yes, that's steam coming up. What do we hear? That's the sound of water boiling. Look, can you see steam? Steam is very, very hot. Can you bounce like you're boiling, too? I have already squeezed the lemons, so I have juice. Let's see what's next.* (Continue following the steps.)

Possible Prompts:

- *Watch as I . . .*
- *Look at the recipe. What do we do next? Then what do we do?*
- *Reread to see where we are.*

■ Step 6: Serve the lemonade (same day)

After the lemonade is cool, enjoy your hard work. Have children try the lemonade and taste the different ingredients. Encourage them to follow the steps to enjoy lemonade at home with their families.

Make It Memorable— Dramatize!

Gestures help students remember the steps, and they add enjoyment. They lead to engagement and learning (Chauhan, 2004; Royka, 2002), especially for English language learners (Sun, 2003).

Gestures can be simple but should be consistent. Match the activity with exaggerated hand and facial movements. Practice often and don't forget to set up a signal to stop!

Integrate the experience

Provide opportunities for students to put things in sequence and practice vocabulary.

■ WRITING CONNECTION: Write a Class "1, 2, 3" book (2–3 days)

Whole-class books provide the model for individual how-to books. Select a task to write about (e.g., making crackers and cheese) or choose a task that children know how to do (e.g., making playdough). The model for writing the book is straightforward:

1. Think about what you know about the task.

2. Break the task into little parts.

3. Tell it step by step.

After a student acts out the task, chart the steps. The next day, transfer the steps on the chart to sheets of the How-to Paper reproducible to create a 1, 2, 3 big book. Reread it often. The name refers to the structure of the book: steps 1, 2, and 3 in order. Number each page of the book and reinforce transitional words. As you and students read the completed book, have them act out each step.

Spotlight on Nonfiction Strategies

✳ Navigate through text features: read captions

✳ Read procedural text: follow a sequence

✳ Understand vocabulary in context

WHAT THIS SOUNDS LIKE

We did a great job following the recipe for lemonade. Now let's write a step-by-step guide for something else we know how to do. We are all experts at some things already! We can teach others to borrow a library book (you do it every week) or get a hot lunch (some of you do that every day). Think about what you know, then break it into little parts, and tell it step by step.

Let's write about getting a hot lunch. Can someone come up here and act it out? We'll watch and name what you do. (Child acts out task.) *Oh look, first Susie picked up a tray. Now what is she doing? Yes, she is putting food on her tray. Next, she's handing in a ticket to the lunch lady. Last, she's sitting down to eat. Good job, Susie! Let's make a 1, 2, 3 chart of what you did.* (Retell the steps and then record them on the chart.) *Read the steps with me. Now let's act them out and see if we left anything out. Do the steps make sense? Tomorrow I'm going to take this chart of our steps and turn each step into a page of a book. We'll call our big book* How to Get a Hot Lunch. *You are such great teachers!*

Possible Prompts:

- *Think about what comes first, next, last.*
- *Does this make sense?*
- *This is step 1. What is step 2?*
- *Did we leave anything out? Did we put in anything extra?*

For a longer immersion (one to two weeks), ask children to brainstorm what they can teach from their daily experiences in school or at home, and write the steps on How-to Paper reproducibles to create their own books.

Examples of how-to topics written by children might include how to make a cupcake, pack a bag, walk a dog, and pitch a baseball.

> ### Tip: Finding Topics
>
> ✔ Think about what children can teach. What do they already know how to do (e.g., put away toys at school, swim after school)? Enlist home help by asking families to send in a list of some activities their child enjoys doing. Even five-year-olds know how to do a lot!

■ Lesson Extension Activities

REVIEW TRANSITIONAL WORDS IN CONTEXT (ONGOING)

Help transitional words become commonplace by using them in the daily schedule and when retelling stories. When we hear our students say, "What are we doing *next*? What's the *last* thing before lunch?" we hear them integrating transitional words.

CONTINUE WHOLE-CLASS HOW-TO EXPERIENCES WITH MORE RECIPES (ONGOING)

Try other easy recipes to learn procedural text; for example, making popcorn, playdough, rock candy, cheese and crackers, or a pinecone bird feeder.

REORDER STORIES USING PICTURES (2 OR MORE DAYS)

Copy three or four key parts of familiar storybooks. Put the corresponding number on the back of the copy to indicate its placement in the story. Then have students re-sequence the book. Organize the pictures and ordered parts into small plastic bags for retelling.

■ Check in to Evaluate

- Can students follow steps in a sequence?
- Can students skim a text to find information?
- Do students use transitional words?

■ Home-School Connection

You can bet that your students will be talking about the fresh lemonade they made in class. That's great! Even when parents cook with their children, they don't always see opportunities for learning. Repeated experiences help students follow a sequence and demonstrate that directions are a part of our lives.

The parent letter extends students' enthusiasm for following directions in a sequence by giving families ideas for more activities. When the opportunity arises, do the following to involve families:

- Invite parents to manage a weekly or monthly how-to center or station.
- Send home how-to activities, such as how to make paper airplanes.

> ## Successful Differentiation
>
> **Supports:**
> - Use photographs to make a how-to book.
> - Act out the steps in making lemonade.
>
> **Challenges:**
> - Re-sequence lemonade recipe.
> - Write a how-to book called *Making Lemonade*.

◼ Reproducibles

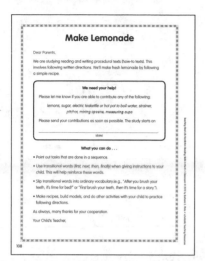

PARENT LETTER (Here is a quick note to send to parents about making lemonade. You'll want to rally their support in bringing in supplies and introducing students to procedural texts.)

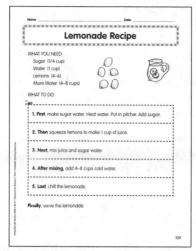

LEMONADE RECIPE

HOW-TO WRITING PAPER (Remind children to refer to the transitional words on this sheet as they write the steps.)

Make Lemonade

Dear Parents,

We are studying reading and writing procedural texts (how-to texts). This involves following written directions. We'll make fresh lemonade by following a simple recipe.

We need your help!

Please let me know if you are able to contribute any of the following:

lemons, sugar, electric teakettle or hot pot to boil water, strainer, pitcher, mixing spoons, measuring cups

Please send your contributions as soon as possible. The study starts on

_____.

(date)

What you can do . . .

- Point out tasks that are done in a sequence.

- Use transitional words (*first, next, then, finally*) when giving instructions to your child. This will help reinforce these words.

- Slip transitional words into ordinary vocabulary (e.g., "*After* you brush your teeth, it's time for bed!" or "*First* brush your teeth, *then* it's time for a story.").

- Make recipes, build models, and do other activities with your child to practice following directions.

As always, many thanks for your cooperation.

Your Child's Teacher,

Teaching Real-Life Nonfiction Reading Skills in the K–1 Classroom © 2013 by Barbara S. Pinto • Scholastic Teaching Resources

Lemonade Recipe

WHAT YOU NEED:

Sugar (1/4 cup)

Water (1 cup)

Lemons (4–6)

More Water (4–8 cups)

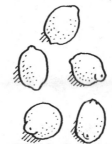 

WHAT TO DO:

1. First, make sugar water. Heat water. Put in pitcher. Add sugar.

2. Then squeeze lemons to make 1 cup of juice.

3. Next, mix juice and sugar water.

4. After mixing, add 4–8 cups cold water.

5. Last, chill the lemonade.

Finally, serve the lemonade.

How-to Paper

How to make: _____

Caption: _____

Step [ ]

_____

_____

_____

_____

_____

First   Then   Next   After   Last   Finally

Chapter 8

Words Inspire Celebrations: Investigate Invitations

Children learn how to find information while they read and write invitations.

A Quick Look at Chapter 8

THE ADVENTURE	Study sample invitations and use these as models to create invitations.
READING WORK	Read invitations and other forms of mail. Learn to read "question words."
WRITING CONNECTION	Write individual invitations.
LEARNING EXTENSION ACTIVITIES	Reread key question words. Study other forms of mail. Create a classroom communication system.
CONTENT-AREA WORK	Key Concepts of an Invitation/Post Office Study: • What are the important parts of an invitation? • Why do people write and send invitations? • What are some ways that people communicate? • How does a post office work?
PACING	12–15 days

Nonfiction Skills for This Adventure

- **Generate and Apply Background Knowledge**
- **Learn and Apply Vocabulary**
- **Group Information**
- **Deepen Understanding**
- **Research**

Why Are We Doing This?

When I was six, my dad arrived home at a regular time every day and picked up the mail. I would immediately ask, "Any mail for me?" "No, just bills" was always his reply. Then one day he threw an envelope in my lap; I had received my first party invitation! I was thrilled and will remember that day forever!

Children can't wait to receive mail! I remember my family reading invitations together. It was great fun finding the perfect birthday invitations to send, or in more ambitious times, making them ourselves.

In this adventure, we look at real mail that children intrinsically want to read. We read mentor invitations to study their essential parts so that children can create their own invitations independently. In addition, they learn to use key question words (*who, what, when, where, why*) in context.

COUNTING THE DAYS

What you need

MATERIALS

✔ Books:

- Nonfiction read-aloud selection: *We Need Mail Carriers* by Lola Schaefer
- Fiction read-aloud selection: *A Letter to Amy* by Ezra Jack Keats
- Other related literature: Look for realistic settings—urban or rural—and for photographs and relevant details, such as the following examples:

  Dear Mr. Blueberry by Simon James

  The Jolly Postman by Allan Ahlberg

  E-Mail by Larry Dane Brimner

✔ Reproducibles:

- Parent Letter, p. 121 (1 copy for each family)
- Invitation Template, p. 122 (display copy and 1 copy for each student)
- Invitation Checklist, p. 123 (display copy and 1 copy for each student)

✔ Other Materials:

- a variety of invitations from families
- posterboard
- baskets of invitations, postcards, greeting cards, and other forms of mail
- chart paper and marker
- sticky notes
- supplies for making invitations: paper, stickers, pens and colored pencils

Teaching Real-Life Nonfiction Reading Skills in the K–1 Classroom © 2013 by Barbara S. Pinto • Scholastic Teaching Resources

PREPARATION

✔ Several weeks before

- *Copy the Parent Letter reproducible and send home with each student.*

✔ 1 week before:

- *Prepare stopping points in literature:* Flag places in *We Need Mail Carriers* that show the mail is moving forward to help children see the sequence of events involved in delivering the mail.

✔ 1 day before:

- *Display a board on which to hang invitations.*
- *Create a Question Words chart for the words* Who? What? Where? When? Why?
- *Make copies of the Invitation Template and Invitation Checklist.*

Tips

✔ Not every child may be able to bring in an invitation, so accept group invitations, such as school flyers. Save mentor invitations from past studies to display.

FUELING UP! (ONGOING)

Activities to keep you going

When children have prior experience with invitations, they are able to read and write their own more easily.

Send and receive class invitations. A few weeks before this study, create situations for sending and receiving invitations; for example, inviting a buddy class for a visit and then receiving a reciprocal invitation from that class. Plan this in advance with fellow teachers. This introduces invitations and the words that commonly appear on them and teaches children how this type of text works, how invitations look, and why they are important.

Browse baskets of invitations. As invitations arrive, place them in baskets so they are easily accessible for students to explore at snack or center time. Set up a daily routine to look at new invitations as they arrive and to compare them to the other invitations. Give students plenty of opportunities to flip through the invitations and read them informally.

Spotlight on Nonfiction Strategies

✳ Activate prior knowledge
✳ Preview the text

Ready to launch

■ Set a Real-Life Purpose (1 day)

This invitation study can stand by itself or dovetail with a content-area study. Decide on an event to celebrate, such as a book fair, a "rock museum" for a geology study, a publishing party for a writing unit, and so on. Think about what's happening in your class and celebrate it! Set a date about a week away, schedule a time, and mark it on the class calendar.

Explain to students that an invitation asks people to attend a celebration, such as a birthday or another important event. Share details about your upcoming celebration and ask children to whom you should send invitations (e.g., teachers, other classes, and/or parents).

Spotlight on Nonfiction Strategies

✷ Connect with a topic
✷ Activate prior knowledge
✷ Generate vocabulary
✷ Question and comment
✷ Preview the text

WHAT THIS SOUNDS LIKE

Boys and girls, we are almost ready to publish our nonfiction stories! You are such great writers, so let's have a celebration and invite our principal. Remember the invitations we sent and received from our buddy classes? We'll send an invitation to tell the principal when and where our celebration will be held.

■ Read Aloud to Explore Writing and Sending Invitations (2 days)

NONFICTION TO READ ALOUD: *WE NEED MAIL CARRIERS* (1 DAY)

Before reading, discuss the types of mail that children have received. Talk about how this mail is delivered to them. Connect this to your upcoming celebration. As you read, stop at the places you flagged in the text to show various jobs portrayed and what is happening to the letter. Highlight how each stage brings the mail closer to the person it's addressed to. After reading, discuss how mail is delivered through the postal system. Remind students that this is how invitations arrive at their homes. Talk about other ways in which mail can be sent (hand-delivered, online).

WHAT THIS SOUNDS LIKE

Before reading: *Have you ever received an invitation in the mail, or a letter or postcard? Have you ever seen or visited a post office? I'm going to read a book that tells and shows what happens after you put a letter in a mailbox. Many people, such as mail carriers, help invitations and other mail get to us. Later, we'll be mail carriers and deliver our publishing party invitation to the principal.*

During reading: *Look at all the different jobs it takes to deliver the mail.* (Name each job.)

After reading: *Do you know that mail gets sent in many ways? The post office is one way, but letters and packages can also be delivered to our doors* (e.g., UPS, courier services) *or sent online. Have you ever used a computer to send mail?*

Possible Prompts:

- *Where is the mail now?*
- *What's happening in this picture?*
- *Do you see how many people help deliver our mail?*

FICTION READ-ALOUD: *A LETTER TO AMY* (1 DAY)

This story tells the tale of Peter's invitation to Amy and his attempts to mail it. During the read-aloud, stop and notice that invitations are a way to let people know about a special event. Review the story by talking about how Peter showed he cared by sending an invitation to Amy.

LIFT OFF! (6–8 DAYS)

Begin the adventure

Create invitations to augment the ones students bring in.

■ Step 1: Display and discuss invitations (1 day)

Set out the display board of invitations that children have informally looked at. During class discussion, look at the display to name the important elements of an invitation.

WHAT THIS SOUNDS LIKE

Look at all the invitations we've collected! Aren't they pretty? What do you notice about how the invitations look? Remember to look at this board when you come to school after you unpack, or at snack time.

Possible Prompts:

- *Where do you see writing?*
- *What does the writing or art tell us?*
- *What else do you see on the invitations?*
- *How do the invitations look alike? How are they different?*

■ Step 2: Create a chart (1 day)

Ask pairs to discuss the parts of an invitation that impart necessary information and additional elements that might appear. Record this information in a T-chart like the one on p. 116. Keep it on display for the duration of this study. If you set up an invitation center later, display the chart there.

Spotlight on Nonfiction Strategies

- ✳ Predict based on prior knowledge
- ✳ Understand dominant features
- ✳ Generalize information
- ✳ Classify information
- ✳ Categorize information
- ✳ Question and comment
- ✳ Infer the known from the unknown
- ✳ Skim for information

AN INVITATION MUST HAVE:	AN INVITATION CAN HAVE:
Who (person giving event or party) What (event or party) When (time/date) Where (place) Why (reason for event or party)	Pictures Things to bring Other information: Bring presents R.S.V.P (tell whether you're coming)

Explain that many invitations have pictures and R.S.V.P. information, and can even contain cartoons or quotes. Emphasize the importance of first including the essential information on an invitation. Then less essential elements can be added to "fancy it up."

WHAT THIS SOUNDS LIKE

Tell your partner which information appears on all invitations. Let's look at one together to notice what it tells us. (Read invitation and note question words.) *The important information on an invitation tells who, what, when, where, and why. Let's make a chart to list what an invitation needs and also what extra stuff it can include. We can use the information in this chart as a model to make an invitation to our publishing party.*

Possible Prompts:

- *What important information do you see on this invitation?*
- *Do I need to know this information? Would I know what to do if this information were missing?*
- *Find the place that tells who the celebration is for. What is being celebrated? When is the celebration? Where is it?*
- *Notice words that tell us* when. *Look for the words* date *and* time.
- *Notice words that tell us* where. *Look for the word* place.

■ Step 3: Explore the print and layout of invitations (1–2 days)

Focus students' attention on the display board of invitations and notice the places where words appear on them. With practice, children recognize that invitations have a unique layout and that they may need to search for information on a page. (Also see the newsletter adventure in Chapter 4.)

WHAT THIS SOUNDS LIKE

Reading an invitation is like putting together a story. We have to look for the parts that go together! Do you see that the words are in different places on the invitations? Readers sometimes have to look in different places on the invitations to find all the words. It may look like a list. (Point to some words.) *Where else do you see words on the invitation?*

■ Step 4: Read invitations to find essential words (1–2 days)

After children become accustomed to how invitations look, introduce them to the words they're most likely to see (*who, what, when, where, why*). We want students to be able to get information easily from an invitation, although there may be lots of print and confusing graphics. Text may appear in different fonts and sizes, and be splattered in many different places. In order to find out what we need to know, we have to extract key words. This process is called skimming. With children, look at the displayed invitations and use the words *who, what, when, where, why* as your guide to finding key pieces of information. Remind students that these question words fit together to make a whole "story." Display the Question Words chart in the classroom.

WHAT THIS SOUNDS LIKE

To find the key words we need, we can skim an invitation. (Refer to Chapter 7 on making lemonade if you've completed that adventure: *Remember that we skimmed when we read our lemonade recipe.*) *Let's try skimming an invitation. An invitation answers some questions about an event. It tells us <u>who</u> is giving the event, <u>what</u> the event is, <u>when</u> and <u>where</u> it takes place, and <u>why</u> the event is taking place. If we want to know when the event or party is, we look for a date and a time. If we want to know <u>where</u>, we look for a place. This Question Words chart shows the words that an invitation answers. This invitation shows <u>why</u> on the front: it's a birthday party.*

Possible Prompts:

• *Look down the invitation and find the word* when *or* where.

• *Do you see words that look like a date?*

• *Look for a month word and numbers, like the ones on our calendar.*

■ Step 5: Create a class invitation (1 day)

Ask children to work with you to create an invitation to the upcoming celebration. Students decide which information to include, generalize what they know about invitations, and figure out what they need to include. Remind students to refer to the Invitations Must Have chart. Set up the display copy of the Invitation Template. Use it to fill in the important details of the event. Finally, consult a display copy of the Invitation Checklist to make sure that the invitation is complete.

WHAT THIS SOUNDS LIKE

Let's create an invitation asking Principal Silver to come to our publishing party. Our Invitation Must Have chart tells us what important information we must include. Then we'll record the information about our publishing party on our Invitation Template.

Who is our celebration for? Yes, it's for us! What kind of event or celebration is it? It's a party. Why are we celebrating? We are publishing our nonfiction stories. What else should we tell Principal Silver? Yes, we need to tell her where the party will be: in our classroom. We can also call that "place." Let's look down the list on our chart and our template and see what other important information we need to add. (Repeat until all parts of the invitation have been completed.) *We'll use this Invitation Checklist to make sure we've included all the important information.*

Possible Prompts:

• *What other information do we need to add?*

• *Is this information complete?*

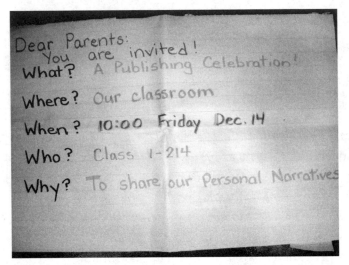

Sample classroom invitation

■ Step 6: Deliver the invitation (1 day)

Deliver the invitation to the recipient by hand, or let the class take it to the mailbox. Many students have never mailed anything and do not realize what happens to an invitation once it is sent, so it helps them to see the process!

Ask the recipient to give feedback about the invitation. At school, there are usually people willing to make positive comments about children's work, so enjoy the praise and use it to inspire more invitations from students.

Integrate the experience

Review and reinforce the language and layout of invitations.

Spotlight on Nonfiction Strategies

* Understand dominant features
* Generalize information
* Categorize information
* Infer the known from the unknown

■ WRITING CONNECTION: Write Invitations (1–2 days)

Writing individual invitations is a natural extension to this reading adventure, and at this point, students are ready for independence. Refer to the class invitation first to review its important parts. Also, review the display board of invitations.

Then distribute copies of the Invitation Template and Invitation Checklist reproducibles to students. Ask them to think of something they'd like to celebrate and to create an invitation for it. Remind children of the supports around them they can consult, including the display board and baskets of invitations and charts.

■ Learning Extension Activities

PROVIDE REPEATED EXPOSURE OF KEY QUESTION WORDS (ONGOING)

* Add new vocabulary to your word wall.
* Enlarge your favorite invitation and display it as a reminder of the question words.
* Conduct word searches for the question words.
* Highlight question words in daily shared and independent reading.
* Encourage students to use correct spelling of these words in their daily writing.

STUDY OTHER FORMS OF COMMUNICATION (2 DAYS)

Encourage students to write in other forms, such as birthday and thank-you cards, letters, and postcards. Set up a communication center with mentor texts and writing tools.

CREATE A CLASSROOM MAILBOX SYSTEM (ONGOING)

To help students become better writers, give them reasons to write! Creating a mailbox in the classroom encourages communication in a fun way! Your class can create and send invitations for many purposes: puppet shows, readers theater, class plays, sharing songs, and more casual events. When you set up mailbox systems within the class, your children have opportunities to create more forms of communication, including the following:

* Friendly letters to friends
* Letters to pen pals
* Greeting cards, including birthday, thank-you, and get-well cards.

■ Check in to Evaluate

1. Do students use and read question words?

2. Can students find information on different parts of the invitation?

3. Can students distinguish between necessary information on an invitation and decorative elements?

■ Home-School Connection

We want our children to take an interest in words, and invitations contain words that matter. Other forms of communication, such as thank-you cards, birthday cards, and letters, are also authentic forms of writing practice. This practice can start at home, even before school begins! The Parent Letter encourages families to read invitations and other appropriate forms of mail with their children and encourages them to create their own invitations at home, too. When the opportunity arises, you can also involve families in the following activities:

• Invite parents to lead an invitation station to create invitations.

• Ask parents to collect blank cards to use for invitations and greeting cards.

Successful Differentiation

Supports:

• Use a template to create an invitation.

• Use mentor invitations to make your own.

Challenges:

• Design templates for invitations.

• Invite parents to visit the school Web site.

■ Reproducibles

PARENT LETTER (This is a quick note to send home to parents about the Investigate Invitations adventure. Families are asked to contribute different kinds of invitations.)

INVITATION TEMPLATE

INVITATION CHECKLIST

Invitations

Dear Parents,

We are studying invitations to continue appreciating words all around us. We are collecting invitations and making our own!

We need your help!

Please look for ALL kinds of invitations, including those for parties, workshops, fairs, sales, openings, book talks, and so on. Please send them in as you find them until _____.

(date)

These invitations can be filled in or blank, but we will NOT be sending them back to you, so please don't send in any that you still need.

What you can do . . .

• Encourage family members to write to your child; read any mail that is addressed to him or her together.

• When an invitation arrives, see if your child can recognize the key words on it, or find the information that tells: Who? What? When? Where? Why?

• Feeling adventurous? Have your child create the invitation for the next event you're planning.

• Read books such as *Dear Mr. Blueberry* and *The Jolly Postman* with your child to practice reading letters.

As always, many thanks for your cooperation.

Your Child's Teacher,

Invitation Template

Who: _____

What: _____

When: _____

Where: _____

Why: _____

Things to bring: _____

Can You Come? ☐ YES   ☐ NO

Invitation Checklist

Read your invitation.

Do you tell . . .

 ☐ Who?

 ☐ What?

 ☐ When?

 ☐ Where?

 ☐ Why?

What extra information did you add? _____

_____

Closing Thoughts:

Teaching Nonfiction in a Natural Way

The role of a teacher gets harder each day, and the responsibility associated with teaching keeps growing. Increasingly, we are asked to be accountable for—and to justify—our educational choices. I believe that teachers are instinctively wise, but now, more than ever, we need to verify it! For this reason, I have consciously built in skills, strategies, book sources, charts, and a research base for the nonfiction work included in this book.

Even so, this is ultimately not my real reason for writing this book. My primary goal is to encourage teachers to play with real-life scenarios and foster true-to-life reading. We *know* that nonfiction work matters. Now it's time to create the most authentic, fun-loving situations to perpetuate that work and foster a love of reading about the natural world in your children.

I hope *Teaching Real-Life Nonfiction Reading Skills in the K–1 Classroom* serves as your springboard. Use it as a first step to create your own adventures while, at the same time, providing fundamental nonfiction work for your youngest learners. Most of all, take pleasure in the rich learning life you're providing for your students. And have fun with it!

References

CHILDREN'S LITERATURE CITED

Chapter 1: Teaching Nonfiction Reading and Writing
Cannon, J. (1993). *Stellaluna*. San Diego: Harcourt Brace Jovanovich.
Ryder, J., & Cherry, L. (1982). *The snail's spell*. New York: F. Warne.

Chapter 2: Word Hunt Walk
Arnold, T. (1998). *The signmaker's assistant*. New York: Dial Books for Young Readers.
Bauer, D. (2006). *Signs*. Bloomington, MN: Yellow Umbrella Books For Early Readers.
Crews, D. (1998). *Night at the fair*. New York: Greenwillow Books.
Hoban, T. (1983). *I read signs*. New York: Greenwillow Books.
Milich, Z. (2002). *City signs*. Toronto: Kids Can Press.
Searcy, J. (2006). *Signs in our world*. London: DK Children.

Chapter 3: Sort Healthy Snacks
Gibbons, G. (2008). *The vegetables we eat*. New York: Holiday House.
Grossman, R. D. (2009). *Eating the rainbow (babies everywhere)*. New York: Star Bright Books.
Palatini, M., & Davis, J. F. (2004). *Sweet tooth*. New York: Simon & Schuster Books for Young Readers.
Rockwell, L. (2009). *Good enough to eat: A kid's guide to food and nutrition*. New York: Harper Collins.
Sharmat, M., Aruego, J., & Dewey, A. (2009). *Gregory, the terrible eater*. New York: Scholastic.

Chapter 4: Create a School Newsletter
Gibbons, G. (1987). *Deadline! From news to newspaper*. New York: Crowell.
Leedy, L. (1990). *The furry news: How to make a newspaper*. New York: Holiday House.
Pilkey, D. (1999). *The paperboy*. New York: Scholastic.
Wood, G. (2010). *The newspaper king*. Mustang, OK: Tate Publishing.

Chapter 5: Use a Map on a School or Neighborhood Treasure Hunt
Elliott, R. (2004). *On a treasure hunt*. Melbourne: Barrie Publishing.
Flint, D. (1998). *Our book of maps*. Crystal Lake, IL: Rigby.
Hartman, G., & Stevenson, H. (1993). *As the crow flies: A first book of maps*. New York: Aladdin.
Rhys, D. (2001). *Reading maps*. New York: Newbridge Educational Publishing.
Sweeney, J., & Cable, A. (1998). *Me on the map*. New York: Dragonfly Books.

Chapter 6: Plant a Salad
Bruce, L., & Beardshaw, R. (2001). *Grow flower, grow!* New York: Scholastic.
Ciciano, J. (2003). *My bean plant*. Washington, DC: National Geographic Society.
Cutting, B., & Cutting, J. (1992). *Seeds, seeds, seeds*. New York: Applecross.
Gibbons, G. (2008). *The vegetables we eat*. New York: Holiday House.
Graham, P. (2002). *Big red tomatoes*. Washington, DC: National Geographic Windows on Literacy.
Hall, Z., & Halpern, S. (1998). *The surprise garden*. New York: Scholastic.
James, S. (2002). *Dolphins*. New York: Mondo Publishing.
King, M. (1995). *Animal eaters of the pond*. New York: Wright Group.
McCormick, R. (2004). *Eat your vegetables!* Parsippany, NJ: Celebration Press.
Sharp, Z. (2004). *This food grows here*. Washington, DC: National Geographic Society.

Chapter 7: Make Lemonade
Frazee, M. (2006). *Walk on! A guide for babies of all ages*. Orlando, FL: Harcourt Publishing.
French, C. (2002). *Make a paper airplane*. Pelham, NY: Benchmark.
Lucero, J. A. (1996). *How to make salsa*. New York: Mondo Publishing.
Oldfield, S., & Curtain, M. (2003). *Making a picture*. Northborough, MA: Sundance.
Pritchett, J. (2004). *How to make a paper frog*. Washington, DC: National Geographic Society.

Chapter 8: Investigate Invitations

Ahlberg, A. (2001). *The jolly postman*. New York: LB Kids.

Brimner, L. D (2000). *E-mail*. Danbury, CT: Children's Press.

James, S. (1996). *Dear Mr. Blueberry*. New York: Aladdin Picture Books.

Keats, E. J. (1998). *A letter to Amy*. New York: Puffin.

Schaefer, L. (2006). *We need mail carriers (helpers in our community)*. North Mankato, MN: Capstone Press.

Additional Resources: Children's Literature

Chapter 3: Sort Healthy Foods

Berenstain, S., & Berenstain, J. (1985). *The Berenstain bears and too much junk food*. New York: Random House.

Canizares, S., & Berger, S. (2000). *Restaurant*. New York: Scholastic.

Evers, C. L. (2006). *How to teach nutrition to kids* (3rd ed.). Portland, OR: 24 Carrot Press.

Food Songs & Nutrition Songs: Teaching Healthy Eating Habits. *Educational Songs & Children's Music from Songs for Teaching*. Retrieved March 3, 2012, from www.songsforteaching.com/foodnutrition.htm.

Free Printables - Worksheets, Kids Nutrition, Food Pyramid, Food Groups, Kids Free Printables. *Nourish Interactive*. Retrieved March 3, 2012 from www.nourishinteractive.com/hco/free_printables.

Leedy, L. (1994). *The edible pyramid: Good eating every day*. New York: Reading Rainbow.

Miller, E. (2006). *The monster health book: A guide to eating healthy, being active & feeling great for monsters & kids!* New York: Holiday House.

Rabe, T., & Ruiz, A. (2001). *Oh the things you can do that are good for you!* New York: Random House.

Turnbull, S., & Haggerty, T. (2006). *Why do we eat?* London: Usborne.

Chapter 4: Create a School Newsletter

Kidblog.org - Blogs for Teachers and Students. *Kidblog.org: Blogs for Teachers and Students*. Retrieved March 16, 2012, from kidblog.org/home.php.

Chapter 5: Use a Map on a School or Neighborhood Treasure Hunt

Aberg, R. (2003). *Map keys*. New York: Children's Press.

Ashley, S. (2005). *I can read a map*. Milwaukee, WI: Weekly Reader Early Learning Library.

Berger, M., & Berger, G. (2004). *Apples/Pumpkins*. New York: Scholastic.

Chesanow, N., & Iosa, A. (1995). *Where do I live?* Hauppauge, NY: Barron's Educational Series.

Cutting, B., & Cutting, J. (1996). *The map book*. Bothell, WA: Wright Group.

Fanelli, S. (1995). *My map book*. New York: HarperCollins.

Heo, Y. (1994). *One afternoon*. London: Orchard Paperbacks.

Leedy, L. (2000). *Mapping Penny's world*. New York: Henry Holt.

Rabe, T., & Ruiz, A. (2002). *There's a map on my lap! All about maps*. New York: Random House.

Ritchie, S. (2009). *Follow that map! A first look at mapping skills*. Toronto: Kids Can Press.

Shores, E. L. (2008). *If maps could talk: using symbols and keys*. Mankato, MN: Capstone Press.

Simon, C. (1999). *Underground train*. New York: Yearling.

Sís, P. (2000). *Madlenka*. New York: Square Fish.

Treays, R., & Wells, R. (1998). *My street*. London: Usborne.

Treays, R., Wells, R., Griffin, A., & Walford, R. (1998). *My town*. London: Usborne.

Wade, M. D. (2003). *Types of maps*. New York: Children's Press.

Weidenman, L. (2001). *What is a map?* Mankato, MN: Yellow Umbrella Books.

Williams, R. L. (1996). *Can you read a map?* Cypress, CA: Creative Teaching Press.

Chapter 6: Plant a Salad

Barrow, J. *Plants we eat*. New York: Scholastic.

Berger, M., & Berger, G. (2007). *Now I know seeds*. New York: Scholastic.

Berger, M., & Berger, G. (2004). *Seed to plant*. New York: Scholastic.

Berger, M. (1995). *The vegetable garden*. New York: Newbridge Communications.

Botanical Interests. Heirloom Seeds. Organic Seeds. www.botanicalinterests.com.

Burpee Gardening. *Burpee Gardening*. www.burpee.com.

Denega, D. (2003). *In the garden*. New York: Scholastic First Discovery.

Direct Gardening Association Garden Catalogs. *Direct Gardening Association: Gardening Companies, Garden Catalogs, Gardening Information*. Retrieved April 6, 2012, from www.mailordergardening.com/catlist. cfm?c=cat4.

Ehlert, L. (1988). *Planting a rainbow*. San Diego: Harcourt.

Flowering Plants | Shrubs | Shade Plants | Garden Plants | Perennials | Spring Hill Nurseries. *Flowering Plants | Shrubs | Shade Plants | Garden Plants | Perennials | Spring Hill Nurseries*. Retrieved April 6, 2012, from www. springhillnursery.com.

Green Plant Escape. *Search of Green Life*. www.urbanext.illinois.edu/gpe/case1/c1a.html.

Halpin, A. (2010). *Plant and garden express: Houseplants for all seasons: A helpful guide*. Naples, FL: Typhoon Media Corporation.

Iversen, S., & Alkema, V. (1994). *A bottle garden*. New York: Wright Group.

Medearis, A. S., & Dubin, J. (1999). *Seeds grow!* New York: Scholastic.

PlantCare.com: Indoor House Plants Database. *PlantCare.com Indoor House Plants Database*. Retrieved April 6, 2012, from www.plantcare.com.

Reeder, T., & Iversen, D. (1997). *Making a garden*. Bothell, WA: Wright Group.

Stutley, A. (1993). *Our garden*. Crystal Lake, IL: Rigby.

Tunkin, D. (2003). *How does my garden grow?*. Washington, D.C.: National Geographic Society.

Walker, C. H. (1992). *Seeds grow*. Bothell, WA: The Wright Group.

Chapter 7: Make Lemonade

Alexander, K. (2007). *Happy hats*. New York: Scholastic.

Dunbier, S., & Gillard, A. (1993). *Making caterpillars and butterflies*. Crystal Lake, IL: Rigby Publications.

Huget, J. L., & Koren, E. (2010). *How to clean your room in 10 easy steps*. New York: Schwartz & Wade Books.

John, V., & Burton, S. (2003). *Hat chat*. Auckland, New Zealand: Shortland Publications

Nichols, J. (2004). *Make a house*. London: Celebration Press.

Pollack, S. (1997). *The mask*. New York: Steck-Vaughn.

Priceman, M. (1994). *How to make an apple pie and see the world*. New York: Knopf.

Vaughan, M. K. (1998). *Parachutes*. London: DK Celebration Press.

Chapter 8: Investigate Invitations

Berger, M. (1994). *Where does the mail go? A book about the postal system*. New York: Discovery Readers.

Gibbons, G. (1986). *The post office book: Mail and how it moves*. New York: HarperCollins.

Greene, C. (1998). *Postal workers deliver our mail (community helpers)*. North Mankato, MN: Child's World Publishing

Kottke, J. (2000). *A day with a mail carrier*. New York: Rosen Book Works.

Macken, J. E. (2003). *Mail carrier (People in my community)* Weekly Reader.

Marshall, V. & Tester, B. (1996). *Postman Pete*. New York: Mondo Publishing

Messinger, R. (2001). *I've got mail!* Lake Hiawatha, NJ: Little Mai Press.

Owen, A. & Thomas, E. (2004). *Delivering your mail: A book about mail carriers*. North Mankato, MN: Picture Window Books

Wells, R. (2004). *Bunny mail: A Max and Ruby lift-the-flap book*. New York: Penguin Group.

USPS.COM. *United States Postal Service*. Retrieved May 1, 2012, from www.usps.gov.

PROFESSIONAL LITERATURE CITED

Anderson, E., & Guthrie, J. T. (1999, April). *Motivating children to gain conceptual knowledge from text: The combination of science observation and interesting texts*. Paper presented to the annual meeting of the American Educational Research Association, Montreal, Canada.

Blachowicz, C., & Ogle, D. (2001). *Reading comprehension: Strategies for independent learners*. New York: Guilford.

Bortnem, G. (2008). Literacy for children in an information age. *Journal of College Teaching and Learning*. Belmont, CA: Wadsworth/Thomson Learning.

Chauhan, V. (2004, October). Drama techniques for teaching English. *The Internet TESL Journal, 10*(10). Retrieved June 14, 2011, from http://iteslj.org/Techniques/Chauhan-Drama.html.

ChooseMyPlate. Retrieved February 16, 2012, from *ChooseMyPlate.gov*. Retrieved February 16, 2012, from www. mypyramid.gov.

Cohen, V. L., & Cowan, J. E. (2008). *Literacy for children in an information age: Teaching reading, writing, and thinking*. Belmont, CA: Wadsworth/Thomson Learning.

Duke, N. K. (2003). Beyond once upon a time. *Instructor* magazine, New York: Scholastic.

Duke, N. K., & Bennett-Armistead, V. S. (2003). *Reading & writing informational text in the primary grades*. New York: Scholastic.

Duke, N. K., & Kays, J. (1998). "Can I say 'Once upon a time'?" Kindergarten children developing knowledge of information book language. *Early Childhood Research Quarterly, 13*(2), 295–318.

Flowers, T. A., & Flowers, L. A. (2009). Nonfiction in the early grades: making reading and writing relevant for all students. *Journal for the Liberal Arts and Sciences, 13*(2), 40–50.

Fountas, I., & Pinnell, S. (2001). *Guided Reading 3–6*. New York: Heinemann.

Mason, J. M., Peterman, C. L., Powell, B. M., & Kerr, B. M. (1989). Reading and writing attempts by kindergartners after book reading by teachers. In J. M. Mason (Ed.), *Reading and writing connections* (pp. 105–120). Boston: Allyn & Bacon.

Monson, D. L. (2012). Reading preferences and self-selected reading. Scott Foresman Leadership Letters. Retrieved July 17, 2012 from www.sfreading.com/resources/pdf/monson.pdf.

Pelligrini, A. D., Perlmutter, J. C., Galda, L., & Brody, G. H. (1990). Joint reading between Head Start children and their mothers. *Child Development, 61*, 443–453.

Royka, J.G. (2002, June). Overcoming the fear of using drama in English language teaching. The Internet TESL Journal, *8*(6). Retrieved June 13, 2011, from http://iteslj.org/Articles/Royka-Drama.html.

Slade, S. (2010, June 4). Why fun is important in learning. In "The Answer Sheet" column by Valerie Strauss. Retrieved January 14, 2012, from http://voices.washingtonpost.com.

Sun, P.-Y. (2003). Using drama and theater to promote literacy development: Some basic classroom applications. *The Clearinghouse on Reading, English, and Communication Digest, 187*.

Tipper, M. Why repetition is important. Retrieved November 3, 2011, from http://www.happychild.org.uk.

Venezky, R. L. (1982). The origins of the present-day chasm between adult literacy needs and school literacy instruction. *Visible Language, 16*, 112–127.

Willis, J. (2006). *Research-based strategies to ignite student learning: Insights from a neurologist and classroom teacher*. Alexandria, VA.: Association for Supervision and Curriculum Development.

Wilson, P. T., & Anderson, R. C. (1986). What they don't know will hurt them: The role of prior knowledge in comprehension. In J. Oransano (Ed.), *Reading comprehension from research to practice* (pp. 31–48), Hillside, NJ: Erlbaum.

Additional Resources: Professional Literature

Bisson, C., & Luckner, J. (1996). Fun in learning: The pedagogical role of fun in adventure education. *Journal of Experiential Education, 19*, 108–112.

Duke, N. K., & Armistead, V. S. (2003). *Reading & writing informational text in the primary grades*. New York: Scholastic Teaching Resources.

Fletcher, R., & Portalupi, J. (2001). *Nonfiction craft lessons: Teaching information writing K–8*. Portland, ME.: Stenhouse Publishers.

Harvey, S., & Goudvis, A. (2000). *Strategies that work: Teaching comprehension to enhance understanding*. York, ME.: Stenhouse Publishers.

Hoyt, L., Mooney, M. E., & Parkes, B. (2003). *Exploring informational texts: From theory to practice*. Portsmouth, NH: Heinemann.

Hoyt, L. (2002). *Make it real: Strategies for success with informational texts*. Portsmouth, NH: Heinemann.

Kristo, J. V., & Bamford, R. A. (2004). *Nonfiction in focus: A comprehensive framework for helping students become independent readers and writers of nonfiction, K–6*. New York: Scholastic.

Robb, L. (2003). *Teaching reading in social studies, science, and math*. New York: Scholastic.

Stead, T. (2002). *Is that a fact? Teaching nonfiction writing K–3*. Portland, ME.: Stenhouse Publishers.